# SEEK

# SEEK

## FINDING YOUR TRUE CALLING

RAKESH GODHWANI

PORTFOLIO
PENGUIN

An imprint of Penguin Random House

PORTFOLIO

USA | Canada | UK | Ireland | Australia
New Zealand | India | South Africa | China | Singapore

Portfolio is part of the Penguin Random House group of companies whose addresses can be found at global.penguinrandomhouse.com

Published by Penguin Random House India Pvt. Ltd
4th Floor, Capital Tower 1, MG Road,
Gurugram 122 002, Haryana, India

Penguin Random House India

First published by Random House India 2013



Proceeds from this book will go to IIM Bangalore and The Akshaya Patra Foundation in ISKCON, Bangalore



10 9 8 7 6 5 4 3 2

ISBN 9788184003215

Typeset in Adobe Garamond by Saanvi Graphics, Noida

Printed at Repro India Limited



www.penguin.co.in

MIX
Paper from responsible sources
FSC® C047271

This is a legitimate digitally printed version of the book and therefore might not have certain extra finishing on the cover.

*To all students trying to make sense of their lives*

# Contents

# The Problem

THE DECISION TO WRITE THIS book was not sudden. I always wished to pen a book on making career choices. When I started to prepare for my campus placements in 1996, I realized how little material was available on making or seeking career choices for job seekers, especially between the age group of 18 to 25. I personally was very confused, made my choices from my limited knowledge about the world and by noticing seniors and mentors around me. With time, I enjoyed talking about careers with friends and juniors, assuming the role of a counsellor to many of them. As I progressed in my journey and moved from Wipro to Intel to Qualcomm and finally to my alma mater IIM Bangalore in the last 16 years, I am now on firmer footing than I was. Probably, it is because I took the Plunnge (Godhwani, 2011) into the non-corporate world, having a lot of time to think and best of all, meeting lot of very interesting people who have studied at IIMB in various programmes.

There were a few incidents that finally led me to write this book. In 2008, I quit the corporate world to follow my dream for teaching and setting up the Alumni and Development office at IIMB (a journey which I have published along with 15 other similar cases in a book called *Plunnge*).[1] The first incident which clearly stood out was during a fine October morning in 2011. I was in office and received an email from a student who had attended one of my talks on my book. She wanted to meet me,

[1] www.plunnge.com or www.facebook.com/plunnge

so I gave her time to come over that afternoon. I did remember the student from the talk because she had walked up to me and asked many questions on career choices. Her name was Neha*. When she came that afternoon, she was not the chirpy girl I remembered from my talk. She was all of 22, about to finish her MBA programme after BCom from an institute in Bangalore.

'Sir, I am very confused. The time has come for me to make a career choice as I graduate next year. The companies will start coming for interviews soon and I am not sure which companies to apply for and how to go about seeking the right job,' she began. I had pretty much guessed what the meeting would be about and was mentally prepared. And just like a doctor who diagnoses a patient before the actual treatment, I started to first ask more questions to collect whatever information I could on her history and her thought processes.

She told me that she belonged to a small village beyond Mysore where her dad was an agriculturist. She was probably one of the first in her family who was sent to a big city for further studies. Her family had spent most of their savings on her education and her stay in a shared accommodation. Bangalore is not an easy city to live in. She was also given a scooter so that she could commute easily. The family saw its first gadget besides a TV, when Neha bought a laptop to use for her assignments. Well, she didn't really need one as the college had a computer centre but then, everyone in the college had one. Overall, the tuition fee, accommodation and the entire investment in her MBA programme of two years was approximately 12 lakh rupees. Her family couldn't afford it but thanks to the easy availability of education loans from banks, she was able to pay for all of this. All of 22 years and already a burden of a loan to

* All names of students in this book have been changed to protect their identity

repay on her young shoulders. I knew that this was one of the biggest reasons for her unusual mood that day—the worry was giving her sleepless nights. Suddenly, this little girl was facing the first truth of the big bad world—loans and EMIs.

Evidence suggests that most students avail an education loan these days—especially those who come for the MBA programme. In 2011, the overall amount outstanding given out as education loans was ₹43,801 crore approximately, or 8.5 billion USD.[2] In developed countries, more than 80 percent students avail education loans. India stands at about 5 percent and growing at 20 percent every year. Loans are unbearable burdens on the backs of these young students which wouldn't let them live in peace till they repay them. In Neha's case, given her family's background, she had no other option but get a job as early as possible so she could repay her loan.

She echoed this situation in her own words. 'Sir, if I don't get a job by March, I don't know what I will do to repay the loan. I am so tensed.' I had heard these words before from many students of her age. I have also heard the same words by many people I meet in the corporate sphere too. Loans and EMIs are probably a big factor in people's career choices. The fear of not earning money is compounded by the fear of not being able to repay the loans. There is a very interesting advertisement on FM radio that depicts this—a person calls his friend and asks him if his company has any job opening. The friend is surprised and asks,'Why? You had just started your current job. What happened?' To which the person says,'Better pay, yaar. I have booked an apartment which will be ready only by next year. So my house rent and EMI are killing me. The current

---

[2] Dinesh Unnikrishnan, 'Education loan norms to be reworked to cut bad debt' http://www.livemint.com/Home-Page/3KuNmy8kj9yPvFxS9W5onL/Education-loan-norms-to-be-reworked-to-cut-bad-debt.html

job does not give me enough.' The advertisement was for a real estate company but accurately portrays the job market today. It doesn't matter if the job is good or bad. What matters is the salary and the ability to pay your EMI.

When Neha finished and waited for my opinion, I asked her a few more questions because I was still not sure what her problem exactly was. So I said, 'Neha, I am sure you will get picked up by any company who is coming to your campus. You are one of the brightest students with good marks. You appear confident and are able to communicate well. What exactly is your problem?' She said,'Sir, I know that. I am quite certain that I will get a job in some company. But I am tensed because I don't know if that job will help me make a better choice later.' I was not sure I understood that comment,'What do you mean?' 'Sir, I am told by my seniors that the first job out of campus pretty much determines the rest of your life. So say if I get a job in an IT company in Bangalore, I am afraid that I will not get any other opportunity in a different sector—say a bank—after two years.'

Now this was something I had heard for the first time. So I probed more and found out that many students of her age look at jobs as a '2 year' episode. I will come to this point later on. But the essential problem at hand for Neha was not a simple one. It was complicated and had layers—like an onion. In Neha's case, the first layer of her problem was the loan and the EMIs. The next layer was her apprehension of what sector to choose and it then exposed a lot more layers of undefined levels. If I probed further, I am sure, I would have encountered a layer called 'social acceptance'. At the end of the day, she came from a lower middle class family. Her parents were a key factor in her life and decisions. Being a girl, she would also have to conform to social norms of her community. Very soon, her family would want her to get married and have a family.

Before I began to answer, she revealed another layer of her problem. 'Sir, I read a few books on careers and many of them say that one should follow their heart and find their true calling. What does that mean?' This part of the conversation has always been my favourite. There are two reasons for it. One is that I found my calling of teaching and took a plunge into it. And two, one of my favourite movies *3 Idiots*, which was shot in IIM Bangalore and I was fortunate to see the entire shooting of, talks about the same thing. This matter of 'calling' and 'dreams' and 'passion' is not that difficult to understand. But since it depends a lot on this cute little thing called 'brain' and its unexplained mysteries, it can leave everyone very confused. Not everyone can answer 'what do you love' easily. I have asked this question to many of my friends and peers too. And it is not surprising that many answer 'I really don't know'. I asked Neha the same question and she said she loved painting, but I knew that she couldn't say whether she liked it as a hobby or a passion. So I left the question hanging and asked her if she could make a living out of painting. She said, 'My dad won't allow me to do that.' And I think that is indeed a very valid concern. Some people may brush away dad's opinion saying what matters is what she loves but that is a very idealistic view. Her family is a key part of her decision. Many times, in India especially, families often dictate career choices of their young ones. And Neha is no different. So even if she loves painting, her dad would probably not encourage her to pursue a life of a painter. For his part, he is not wrong to think like that. He has seen a country where painters are not able to make ends meet—not everyone is a M. F. Hussain or a Jatin Das. It requires years of struggle and is not for the faint hearted. Her dad thought that a BCom and an MBA would be a simpler route for his child to be independent and earn money to live a better life. Let's face it—Neha is living her dad's dream as of now. And there is no way that is going to change in the short term. She might have been happier in an arts degree. But her dad guided her into a BCom degree. I'm sure her dad wants the best for her. So his best was defined as BCom and not BA for his daughter. This doesn't mean that BA is not as good as BCom. I think Neha's dad feels and believes that BCom will give her a better opportunity to earn good money as compared to a BA degree. Most parents have only one metric to judge education—the return in monetary terms. So any degree that gives more money as reported by the newspapers that they read, is the best option for their children.

My theory is corroborated by my own uncle, a family friend, who once called me and said that his son is appearing for engineering exams and is 17 years old. He asked me to help him narrow down a list of good colleges where he could apply once he got his scores. I obediently gave him the list I downloaded from some website. Over the next few weeks, we spoke every alternate weekend and I was happy to share whatever I knew about engineering colleges since I went to one of them. Then one day, he informed me that he had shortlisted three colleges in India which he felt were best for his son based on his scores and eligibility. Please note that uptil this moment, his son never called or spoke to me. What a life! Imagine your dad doing everything…Man…I want that life too. Anyway, on the list were three colleges which had one thing in common—80 percent or more placement record of its students. All three of them boasted in their brochures about how their placement offices have relations with top companies of India—mostly the IT sector. And that did it. My uncle applied to these three for his son, and finally settled for the one where the placement record was better than the other two. That seems like an easy enough decision, doesn't it? And my uncle is right. After all, which son, at the age of 17 would be able to understand how the world works? Which child would realize the big bad world at that tender age? And how would they make a decision when, till they grow out of their teens, everything is given to them on a platter by their mom or dad? So after shoving his son into this engineering school that promised a job at the end of four years, my uncle relaxed and announced that his responsibility was over. The process would take over and without a doubt, unless his son does something really stupid, he is guaranteed a job of 30-40k/month in some IT factory in India. That the son is now in touch with me with the same questions as Neha is a different story altogether, and hopefully part of this book's purpose, but it amazes me that our parents pretty much dictate our career choices—talk about modernism and an advansing society.

Coming back to Neha's situation, I could now understand her problem and put it down as below

1. How does one make a career choice that helps one strike a balance between their current responsibilities (loan, parents, social acceptance) and their own space in the world (future prospects, better opportunities etc)?
2. What choices does one have in front of them and how does one make the best choice?
3. What if one doesn't like the job? What does one do then? Is it the end of the road or are there ways to find new opportunities?
4. What is 'calling' and how does one find their true calling? Assuming they do, will they be able to earn a living from that?

Neha left my office quite confused after our meeting. That's because I didn't and wasn't able to give her any satisfactory answers to any of her points above. My answers were very philosophical and I myself was not sure how to allay her fears. I knew most of her thoughts were perceptions—but they were very deep rooted. And I knew that a thirty minute meeting with me wouldn't break them down. Many students have myths about life and careers that dictate their career choices. I will talk more about these in the next chapter.

The other incident that helped trigger this book was when I invited fifteen alumni of IIMB to come and talk to the first year students in their first week on campus. I organize this event every year and they are my favourite days at campus bringing two generations together. The alumni are from various batches—some as old as from the seventies and some as recent as 2005. They belong to all kinds of sectors and represent a cross section of industry in some way. I prefer to maintain a gap of at least 10 years in age because I want the students to see a very different perspective of life and careers through the alumni. My purpose of doing this session with the senior folks is to talk about the following

1. Top three career choices that the alumni made
2. Top three lessons to students from their own career choices
3. Top three mistakes along the way

I personally am awed when I hear the rich stories of these alumni. I am able to relate to the students' view because I interact with them a lot too. In one such session, a young student Suhas asked a very pointed question to one alumnus who was in marketing. 'Sir, how do you find your dream job in marketing? In my case, I have never worked in any company but I like marketing as a subject which is why I opted to do an MBA. But after coming here, my seniors tell me that I should focus on a consulting job that allows me to broaden my prospects. Some say that if I enter a marketing job, I will get posted in a village. And many say that marketing is not the sunshine sector anymore.' The whole audience laughed and some made that irritated sound expressing their displeasure at the long question. I could also make out that 'what a stupid question' sound. The alumni also felt that the question was slightly immature. Suhas was snubbed and his question was buried somewhere in the next line of queries. But I noted 'sunshine sector' and 'dream job of marketing' in his questions and made a mental note to keep track of the pattern of questions. It was as I had guessed. Most other questions that day were broadly on these two points—slightly different in expression but in essence the following

1. How do I keep my future self employable? The sectors lose their shine with time. So how do I prepare myself for a situation that is not at a disadvantage as compared to others?
2. How do I know that I am best suited for a sector, whether marketing, finance, or consulting?

Again, there are hidden layers in these questions. A big concern of students that I saw coming out in that event was their peer standing against each other. I thought that there was a hidden 'I must be ahead of others' in that room that day. There is nothing wrong with that feeling. After all, the MBA programme does give a feeling of competitiveness and the CAT exam is no easy bridge to cross to get into IIMB. So the stakes are quite high and students value peer standing as a key way to define their career choices. It doesn't matter what one likes. But it does matter that one's standing is better than the other. For example twenty years ago, a marketing job was the dream job for an MBA student of India. But now, it is not. That is because the marketing job is perceived to be a lower peer standing than a job in a consulting company or an investment bank. Again, the student may be ideal for a marketing job—she may have interests and qualities that suit marketing. But just because of the social standing, they would rather go for a job in a more acceptable sector which is defined by the words 'sunrise' or 'growing' and with future opportunities galore.

The final incident that triggered this book, besides the lovely invite from my publisher to commission it, was another student of mine from a college where I was a guest faculty. I was done with my class that day and Ravi came to see me. He was a quiet student; he asked me if he could talk to me about some doubts that he had. I asked him to come over to my office after lunch. I had interacted with him earlier on a few occasions. He was one of the eldest in the class with more than five years of work experience before he came for the MBA programme. He was apparently different from the rest of the class as well. He had worked for a manufacturing company and felt that the MBA programme would help him make a bigger leap in his career. His focus was to apply for investment banks or the financial sector because these jobs offer the best remuneration. I was glad to hear that that his aim was to have a job that paid really well. At least he was clear and honest about it. Many students always downplay their ambitions. But Ravi was quite sure. When he came to my office, I asked him if he'd gotten placed as he had written to me saying that he was applying to a few companies. He looked very dejected and blurted, 'Yes sir.'

'You sound as if that's a bad thing. Congratulations. When is the party?'

'Sir, I got a job in ABC—an MNC in the technology sector.'

I realized that his dream of entering an investment bank had gone kaput. Nevertheless, getting into ABC was no small accomplishment. They pay really well too. The job was in the business development side and he could grow really well with time. But he looked tortured. It was as if he was in some special kind of hell.

'What's wrong? If you didn't want this, why did you apply in ABC?' I asked him.

'Sir, the banks and companies where I wanted to apply were coming later. And I was afraid that if I don't get into them, I might lose all the other companies which were coming earlier. So I just applied out of fear of failure to ABC and landed a job. The placement process is stringent. It won't let me apply for another job now,' he lamented.

I felt really sorry for Ravi. Here was a classic example of how fear of failure could make students adopt a poor career choice and then regret it. He was stuck in a rut now. I was convinced, though I didn't show it to him, that he would wait for a year to finish, resign, and then apply to the IBanks or his dream companies. Chances of the investment banks hiring him out of campus are quite low as he is now in a different sector and there are millions like him who apply to these niche companies. So either he has to reconfigure his career path, accept what he has on his plate, and move on or repent for the rest of his life. He is just 28. And I worry that at such a young age, he feels defeated despite having a wonderful opportunity in front of him. I call this Destiny. The more you try and resist it, the more miserable you become. I know many students would give an arm and leg to get Ravi's job. But Ravi just doesn't like it. His heart was set on something else. This brings me to two questions.

1. Why did Ravi have such a bias towards the jobs he felt were the best or to put it bluntly, 'What is the big deal about an investment banking (also called Ibanking) job? Is it just the money that defines a 'wow' job?' Where does that come from and how can students be wary of such episodes?
2. Now that Ravi is in this soup, what are the choices he has for his career? What if he just doesn't like the job at ABC? How does one handle such career situations?

All the three incidents above, along with support from my publisher pushed me to write this book. Thanks to my job as the head of IIMB Alumni Association, my office has a steady stream of alumni from all our programmes. I thoroughly enjoy having conversations with them over steaming hot cups of coffee in the lovely, verdant and serene campus of our alma mater. I enjoy listening to their stories from their graduation day till where they are today. So when I saw these two ends of the spectrum—students on one side asking questions on how to make career choices and alumni who have been there done that, I thought it is only fitting that I pen down a book where they can meet and benefit from each other.

## Dream Job

Stories of Neha, Suhas, or Ravi are not uncommon. You can see many Nehas in a similar situation but in a different context. For example, instead of joining a B school, Neha could have continued at Infosys, gone to the US for an assignment, applied for an MS from—say Berkeley—and still be in the same situation she is today. Or instead of 'Neha the topper', there could be 'Neha the average student' of the class in Mechanical, who wouldn't have good grades to qualify for Infosys in the campus placement. But Neha knows that she wants a job in an IT company and not a trucking or manufacturing company. So Neha just waits for any IT company that shortlists her. Let's call this company XYZ Technologies. Neha could be overjoyed to have an IT job but on joining the company, this company might ask her to work as a consultant at the client's place which could be managing a big server in their office. Her day then would look like this—she would have to go from desk to desk of that company's employees who have IT problems like wi-fi not working, or the keyboard/mouse needing replacement. I am sure, that Neha would be sitting with Confusion right beside her. I am not saying that doing a job like that is menial. All I am suggesting is that Neha's efforts to get a job in a particular company and the actual job she lands in that company are a mismatch which causes a problem for her and the company.

As the head of alumni at IIM Bangalore, I engage with about 10,000 alumni from various programmes settled worldwide. As an Adjunct Professor, I interact with the students, who in a few years will become alumni. I notice their dilemmas on career choices every day. There are about 10 percent in the batch who are very sure of what they want to do in life and know their calling. One can clearly see their focus and confidence. They will mostly bag the most coveted jobs and do well wherever they go.

The remaining students like Neha, though, face a big challenge. They all get jobs based on a placement process that focuses on making sure that everyone gets placed. It doesn't matter if they like it or not. I am told that about 20-25 percent of them make their first change in less than a year of being in that job after they graduate. (This is anecdotal data and may vary across institutes and the economic scenarios.) Most common reason cited by them is 'the role isn't exciting enough'. Within 2-3 years, about half of the batch makes a career change to a different sector or a company. There is peer pressure that if they don't change jobs, the market or the peer group perceives them to be unfit and incapable. After about 5-7 years of leaving campus, though job changes are less frequent but more focussed on either a better pay or a better role in the same sector, they all seem restless. And then, they either start to realize their calling and move towards it, or resign to the fact that it might be too risky or too late. So they'd rather float around, earn the pay check, and slowly vanish from the circles.

Overall, I sense that there is a major thrash in the job market—especially in the age bracket of 18 to 25. No one seems happy. The employers are unhappy as there is huge attrition and the work force is not committed. The students are not happy because they are not sure what their 'dream job' is and there is huge peer pressure to perform well. So, if more than half of the batch is unsure of what they want to do, then this is a huge problem I see for our generation and our country.

**To Put This Problem in Some Mathematical Form, Here is My Take**

Total number of students in various colleges, universities after their 12th in India – 4,85,00,000 (approx. 4.85 crore between the age group of 18 and 23)

Fair share calculation on the number of students eligible for their first jobs – 8,00,000 (approx. 8 lakh)

10 percent leave the job in the first year – 80,000 (approx. 80 thousand)

Loss to the industry (cost of recruitment, training, and productivity) – ₹25,000/month/candidate approximately

Overall loss to the industry – ₹2,000 crore (about 400 million USD) a year—and this is just a guesstimate based on 10 percent churn. If I make it 15 percent or 20 percent, it's still a HUGE loss with few more zeros to it.

Imagine the loss to the country—opportunity cost of that job to someone else + industry loss + using subsidies on educating that candidate + tax payers money + loans + loss to the candidate … I think it is incalculable. And I shudder at this loss.

(Source: Statistics of higher education and technical education 2009-10)

In this book, I have attempted to go towards the side of the students and probe about career choices from their perspective. This word 'calling' is not an easy one to explain and understand from a student's perspective. The students are smart and much more informed than older generations like mine and prior to mine. The world has become extremely competitive. The students are burdened with education loans at a very young age. And in this scenario, if you talk to them and say 'find your calling', they will either think you are mad, or will just not connect with you and your ideas. So it is very important that we try and step into the shoes of this young generation and understand them better. We must try and appreciate how they make career choices and what are the various drivers or factors of making these choices.

Using that as a foundation, I have attempted to carve ten handpicked stories of alumni of IIM Bangalore who have done well for themselves and found their calling. For some it has been a eureka moment, for others more thought out and clinical. I have used their collective experience to provide a framework for the current students to make well-informed career choices which will help them discover their calling.

## The Student's Perspective

While writing this book, I met a lot of students from a range of schools in India—graduate and post graduate. Most of them were from science, commerce, arts, and business backgrounds because I understand this space better than others like medicine and law. My meetings with students were very informal ones—sometimes one on one or sometimes in a focussed group. I highlighted only one point to all of them that my intention was to stay on the question, 'How does a student today make a career choice?' I just let them talk and never attempted to colour their views with what I thought was the right thing to do. The more time I spent with these bright young minds of our country, the more I realized that this generation has really been given a very tough terrain to walk on. Expecting them to make the right moves in this situation is really asking a lot from these young ones. So as a first step to writing the book, I thought I will first highlight this difficult terrain from their point of view.

If you are a person between 18 to 25 years of age, studying in a college of India, you are probably 'seeking' the next phase of your life. And you are not alone. You are also not the first generation to go through this phase. This has been going on for thousands of years. The Vedic scriptures clearly document that the first 25 years of one's life are the 'brahamcharya' period of a person which is what you are in. This number 25 has probably shrunk to 20 or 21 or 22, it doesn't really matter. It is natural for a student to be anxious in this period because this is a period of transition from one phase of life to the next. You are expected to take charge and enter the next phase of life called 'grahasth' where you need to support a household. Your anxiety stems from very basic questions that again are very natural for any normal person to ask like 'what's out there?', 'what is going to happen?', 'what do I do today to be prepared for that phase?' etc. Five thousand years ago, there were fewer people and fewer options which, again, were very well defined. One either chose knowledge as a path for the next phase of life, or army, business, or labour—also known as the Brahman, Kshatriya, Vaishya, or Shudra—the Varnas of the society. Making a decision on what to choose from the four jobs above was relatively easy—one had to demonstrate a skill that corresponded to these types of classifications. But very soon, the system became very rigid and with time, defined a society that accepted the Brahmins as the highest in the pecking order and Shudra's the lowest. Thus was born the caste systems of our country which defined a person and his profession based on what parentage one was born into. So the son of a Vaishya became a Vaishya and so on.

Today's times are very different and much more complicated. With an education system that is highly competitive, a population of 1.2 billion, and a country which is still finding its feet while being expected to run—this young generation has the following major problems to deal with while seeking their careers

1. Parents dictating every move
2. Financial burdens
3. Social and peer pressure
4. Information gaps
5. Myths, biases, and prejudices
6. Hierarchical systems and pecking orders
7. Fear of failure

Let's take a look at each of these problems from a student's perspective and understand how they impact their career choices.

## *Parents dictating every move*

Someone rightly said that one can't choose one's parents or bosses. So it is best to make peace with that and move on. Having said that, parents only want their children to do well and many times impose their decisions on the children… I am a parent too. I take it as my responsibility to ensure that my children are on the path which I, as a parent, feel is best for them. But there will come a time when they are ready, and when that moment comes, I as a parent must step back.

Allow me to explain what I mean by 'stepping back' by an example from *Finding Nemo*—one of my favourite movies.

In *Finding Nemo*, a small clown fish Nemo is the only child of his father—Marlin. Marlin is super protective of Nemo, and won't let him do anything except what he thinks is best. Nemo gets so bugged with his dad's 'do this, don't do that' attitude that he revolts and swims beyond the reef into the ocean, gets captured by a swimmer, and is taken to Sydney. Marlin swims all the way to rescue him and braves different kinds of adventures along the way. In one such adventure, Marlin meets Crush—a giant 150-year-old turtle. Crush is very different as a parent from Marlin. He teaches his son Squirt how to swim and lets him be. While they are swimming in this big wave called the East Australian Current, Squirt falls out of the current and is in danger of being left behind from the group. Marlin rushes to save him but Crush stops him and says, 'Let's see what Squirt does. He may be a child but this is how he will learn to grow up.' After a couple of tense moments, Squirt finds his way back into the current and is jubilant. Crush congratulates him and encourages him further. Marlin is spellbound. He asks Crush, 'How do you know that children grow up and when to let them be?' Crush responds very philosophically, 'When they know, you'll know.' Marlin then transforms into a parent who lets Nemo do what he wants, lets him choose his own path, and they all lived happily ever after. The moral of the story is quite simple—stop treating your children as kids all the time. Teach them how to swim and then let them be. In other words, let's give our children good education. Then, let them figure out what they want to do in life. Let's trust their judgement and encourage them to take their own decisions.

Parents are one of the biggest influencers in career choices for students. In India, a lot of parents also decide who their children get married to, what jobs they take, and what is best for them in every walk of life. In my meetings with many students over the last four years, a big reason for a student to be where he is today is because of their parent's choice. Now, parent's decision systems are at least one generation behind the current times. So if today the country is ready to have dancers, singers, hair stylists, cooks as respectable professions, they will still force their children to become doctors or engineers or something which relates to a handful of choices from the careers of their generation. The conflict of 'dream' and 'calling' starts at home for this generation. Consequences of this can be devastating. The student typically will end up doing something that his parent thinks is best but may not be true in today's times. That is the reason majority of students in engineering and medical schools don't enjoy being engineers or doctors. When one doesn't enjoy what they do, they translate into a very poor workforce. One then always has a hidden dream which is restrained by parents, gets buried with time but still lurks and erupts in future as they grow more mature. This causes major angst among the young and many of them live with a lifelong grudge in their hearts.

## *Financial burdens*

Education is big business now. In a survey done on Indian families, they are asked a very simple question—'If you had one lakh rupees today as a gift, how would you spend it?' Every year, one of the answers in the top 10 choices of these families is 'investing in education for our children'. Given this dynamic, education is now one of the most talked about sectors to invest in for anyone and everyone. My parents got education virtually free and I too in some sense paid almost nothing—thanks to the government control and utilization of the tax payer's money into my fee. I am now paying a fortune for my son's school and I am told that once he turns eighteen, I should be prepared with a pot of gold to have him enter a good college. Since I took the Plunnge and chose happiness over fat pay packets, I probably won't have this pot of gold ready. There are many other families like mine, I'm sure. This is where the banks come in—to provide educational loans for our children so that they can get good education. Now this comes with a price. Banks aren't really charitable organizations. When they give money, they expect to be paid with interest. And to be living a life under an EMI can be quite a burden. Sadly, students have to live with this burden when they are as young as 21.

A loan is not the only financial burden. One must not forget that as India has progressed, our cities have grown bigger. Real estate has become dearer. So to live in a big city, a student coming from a small town either has to buy or rent a place. In either case, a significant portion of one's salary goes in the cost of living in that city—house, conveyance, and food. None of these are cheap. To give you some anecdotal data, one needs approximately ₹15,000 to live in a shared accommodation, travel back and forth from work every day, and eat three meals a day. This is just survival basics. A visit to the mall can set you back by ₹500 easily. And if you have a spouse or children, then you can just keep adding to the costs further.

So a student who is about to enter the grahasth ashram is already burdened with a mountain of financial problems which his parents did not have in their times. An EMI of ₹15,000 per month with the basic survival costs I just mentioned of ₹15,000 per month have already raised the minimum entry level criteria for the student at a job that has to give them at least ₹30,000 per month in hand. This translates to a job that gives them a package of ₹4.5 lakh or more a year. This is the reason why many students always look at salaries as one of the prime motivators of seeking careers. This is also the reason that if you tell them 'money will come, just don't worry', they will probably think you are from a different planet altogether.

### *Social and peer pressure*

The Nehas, Ravis, and Suhases of the generation today are very closely connected to each other through a variety of media. They all compare and share what they have and what they don't have. Each of them tries to stay of the others for want of getting more social attention in the peer group. This is taught to them from their early days and it becomes quite a burden as they all grow and start making decisions on their own. If we take the case of Ravi, his situation of not getting his dream job was clearly driven from peer pressure. When he would have gotten into the prestigious college, say an IIM, his peer ranking went miles ahead of others. And that becomes a burden to maintain. So Ravi will always try to be miles ahead of others by opting for jobs that give him that position. But now, since he could not get into an investment bank which he considered to be the highest in the pecking order of jobs from IIMs, he might spiral in a vicious downward cycle of peer pressure dictating his every move. Society is a very integral part of our lives. We cannot tear ourselves away from it. Strangely enough, the neighbours, friends, relatives, school mates, aunts and uncles in the apartment, extended friend circles all make your career decisions their business which is never pleasant. When I left the corporate world to follow my dream, my peer group did express its scathing remarks. Many of my 'friends' stopped inviting us to their kid's birthday parties. I became a social outcast. I was able to deal with it easily because with time, I realized that it just doesn't matter what my peer group thinks. It's my life after all. They are welcome to express their opinions and I have figured out how to deal with it. However, this may not be a very ideal situation for a young student to be in today. We are social beings. So being an outcast is not something we are designed to tolerate with ease.

Here is an example of how peer pressure can influence career decisions. An MBA student sought some career advice from me. He was a very fun loving, outgoing person. In his college, he was the go-to guy for everyone when there was some trouble. Through his connections, charm, and positive attitude, he could sort out any mess that crops up in typical student scenarios. I advised him to apply for a sales-oriented job, laid out the roadmap, opportunities, and he too concurred that he would be happy in that role rather than a boring desk job which many others in his class were pursuing. He was also aware that sales jobs typically don't pay as well as IT jobs. He applied to two companies and got selected in one of them. Very soon, he was the Area Manager for South India for a company and was dealing with distributors, resellers, customers, and loving every minute of it. He was on the road twenty days a month and had excellent connections in every market in the South. I didn't hear from him after that for a few years. Early in 2012, I got his wedding invite and a message that he had shifted to a top IT company, in a consulting role that required him to sit in office, handle queries from the pre-sales team, and consult within the company for possible suggestions etc. For the life of me, I couldn't figure how this transition happened. After a few months I got a call from him. This time, his tone was somber and I couldn't resist asking him. 'You were doing so well in the sales role. You had also clearly stayed away from IT companies and desk jobs in the campus. So what happened in the two years? Did you hate the sales job?' He said, 'Sir, I loved my sales role. But I was getting married. My parents and my future in-laws didn't like me travelling twenty days a month. So they forced me to move to an IT company. Plus they said that the social acceptance of a job in IT company, no matter how boring it might be, is much higher than a field job of sales.'

I was flabbergasted. This poor guy was made to quit his dreams because of social and familial pressure. He is in touch with me and some weeks back informed me that he will stay in that company for another 1-2 years. His wife has finally agreed to let him travel and he will find a sales profile within the IT company. While I sincerely appreciate his passion to try and do what he likes to do, I hope he realizes that he is not alone anymore. I am sure that he and his wife will have children soon which may change his priorities. He might have to make a choice between being a responsible father and husband and a jet-setting salesman.

The other phenomenon that is important for us to understand is 'herd mentality'. To give you a simple example, we are all familiar by how unruly traffic in India is. Imagine a narrow lane clogged by a stream of traffic. The moment one person jumps the line and drives to the other side, squeezing his way through, the others follow. This is herd mentality. Whether it is wrong or right, it doesn't matter. When you see someone doing it, a natural tendency for many others is to follow. Students also have to deal with this problem. When everyone around them is preparing for an engineering exam by going to coaching classes they will follow too. When parents see their neighbour's child get a good job in IT sector after doing a civil engineering programme at some college, they push their own child there—which is what my uncle wanted for his son. When Salmaan Khan puts his aviator glasses on, we all follow. This is herd mentality. So for a student to suddenly decide that he wants to make his own path, they have to choose between becoming a social pariah or a socially accepted being. In a paper published by professors at IIM Bangalore, they found out that social pressure is one of the big reasons for students to make career choices.[3]

## *Information gaps*

Students get information on careers from a variety of sources, namely

1. Parents, seniors and peer circles
2. Media—TV/Radio
3. Social media and internet
4. Newspapers, magazines, blogs
5. Books, journals
6. Corporate, job providers
7. Educational institutes, teachers, alumni

Students have an information overload on careers today. Each medium and each source has its own opinion and viewpoint. The media are no more conduits of information. They are large corporate houses, organizations, companies which make profits on the business of information. It's their job to put a spin on the medium and make it sellable. So a student wakes up in the morning and reads a newspaper that is full of advertisements or classifieds on jobs from companies. The business section has commentary on how a certain company is not doing too well signifying that the sector is not attractive enough. The television is spewing multiple newsflashes which give a totally different world view as well. A very common onslaught on TV is the advertisements from websites which have become mass portals for jobs, matrimony, buying or selling, etc. Success stories are

[3] 'Social influence and job choice decisions' (Kulkarni & Nithyanand, 2013)

glorified on prime slots, famous leaders are invited to give their view, and the students get influenced by all of this around them. At schools or colleges, their teachers or seniors give them more views, often unsolicited. Students then come back home and log on to social network sites where an inspiring story of how a 21-year-old is now a millionaire by sheer grit is making the rounds. Videos on YouTube now start with advertisements and there is consumerism everywhere. Newest cars, mobile phones, clothes, watches scream out 'buy me' and students realize that a well-paying job is mission critical for their desires to come true. Then there are bits of information with catchy headlines like 'MBA world loses its shine!' or 'Web 2.0—the new frontier for tech jobs'. How in the world would a poor student keep his head above in this water infested with so much information?

Overall, each source of information tends to give variety of views and create gaps in the minds of students. They don't get answers to simple questions from this entire ocean of information. It's like the famous quote 'water water everywhere, not a drop to drink!'

In 2012, there was an article written by a member of a top global audit and consulting company. It was like an open letter from him to all students who were about to enter the corporate world. The article soon went viral and within a few days was the only topic of discussion in many colleges and circles. I read it too. The article commented on how the students should equip themselves with skills, not degrees, to enter the corporate world. Somewhere in the middle of that article, it sounded almost like a headmaster giving a speech to his students on the disciplinary policies of the corporate, what is expected out of them etc. The students expressed a lot of anger at this article and one said to me, 'He himself was a student too. And he must have learnt all that when he worked on the job. So how can he expect a fresh student to behave like a mature 40-year-old executive?' One student commented that it is easy to be on the other side of the table and give lectures to students all the time. When he was a student, he didn't have the challenges that we face today.

I too started to follow this article with extreme interest and in one particular response, I liked how a student wrote back in another 'open letter to the corporate' that if you expect great things out of the students and workforce, you should also motivate them, pay them, and nurture them accordingly. That response also highlighted how the corporate 'milks' its workforce for profits and encourages the people to have the same qualities the article chided. For example no corporate rewards any employee for speaking or writing good English. Students hear stories of their seniors who attempt to ask questions and are made to shut up, they hear how an employee is fired heartlessly despite putting all his life for the company's work, and how they are shoved into boring training programmes expecting them to transform into leaders.

Now if this isn't confusing enough, earlier this month, I saw a wonderful article from *Forbes* on 'Top 5 Regrets of Those Who Are About to Die'. As you might have guessed, the article talks about that most people, before dying, say that they were fools to have worked so hard in the rat race.

Now imagine. One article slaps you, another cajoles you, and the last provokes you. None of these pieces of information actually help you in any way. They just confuse you further. They also make you feel terrible. Would you like to wake up to this situation every day? I know I wouldn't.

## Myths, biases, and prejudices

As I was researching this topic and going around in colleges and universities meeting students, I was struck by how certain myths, biases, and prejudices dictate their career decisions. The simplest myth in front of a 17-year-old and his parents today is that engineering is the shortest and surest way to get a job today as compared to medical, law, etc. It takes four years and by 21, if you are in a decent college, you will probably land a job in IT sector for sure in Bangalore, Pune, Chennai, Hyderabad, or Gurgaon. There are many new cities shaping up as well—Coimbatore, Mohali, Jaipur, Mysore, and so on. Now this myth is backed with enough reports and proof that the model works. So there come feeder systems to this model. Coaching institutes spring open 'guaranteeing' a good rank in the entrance test. So a student or his parents start using basic math to decide that for an investment of ₹10 lakh for four years for an engineering degree, even if you will get a job of ₹3 lakh per annum as a starting point, the student recovers the loan in 3-4 years and is on their way to buy their first car or house. Basically, there is a confirmed myth that engineering route gives security for survival today. This is then drawn backward and students are made to opt for Science and Math in their class 10$^{th}$ or 12$^{th}$ so that they can be effortlessly fed into this system.

I read this particular bias on the Facebook update of a student.

*'IPS is a really tough thingy dude…I mean*

*(1) General Public tumhe kabhi respect degi nahi*

*(2) Gundon se aise bhi nahi banegi tumhari*

*(3) Politicians and neta tumhe aise bhi kuch nahi samjhenge*

*(4) Imaandaar rahoge to colleagues se bhi nahi banegi kabhi*

*fir kya hi faayda IPS ka?'…*

Translated to—*IPS is a real tough career. The general public doesn't respect you, bad guys will anyway be against you, the politicians and beaurocrats will not like you and if you are honest, your own colleagues will not be friendly to you. So what's the point in joining IPS?*

Here we are thinking that students are future leaders. But this is what the reality is. It's not their fault either. It is the bias that they have inherited with education and upbringing that is the problem. Why would this student become an IPS officer and protect his country?

There are many more myths that lurk around in a students' mind today

1. Choose a sunshine sector or avoid a sector that is a sunset sector
2. If the first job is in manufacturing, you will then be stuck in this sector for the rest of your life (and you can replace manufacturing with any other sector)
3. I want to work in a consulting role for two years because that will let me keep my options open for the future
4. Marketing and sales jobs get you posted in villages and rural areas. Finance jobs pay the most
5. If I don't change jobs post-education within two years, I will get stuck in the same sector for life
6. It's better to have a broader horizontal experience in multiple area or topics (both in education or job) rather than an in-depth vertical one on just one area or topic

## *Hierarchical systems and pecking orders*

There is a 'pecking order' amongst students that I found very interesting when talking to them about their choices. It usually comes from reading the 'Top school rankings' studies that are conducted by various agencies and media houses. It works as follows—the top rankers of the exams for any curriculum go to top schools and so on in a pecking order defined by factors like brand of the college, placement opportunities, what the media says about them etc. Basically, students are made to have an order towards their choice of colleges and hence jobs. A topper of an entrance exam will get to choose a top college as she will be on the high pecking order of rank. This makes the life of a student more miserable if they don't do well in the exams and then have to choose a college in a lower pecking order and then be branded as a mediocre student. This phenomenon is made worse by the corporate sector defining a tier system in hiring from the colleges. So colleges like IITs, NIITs etc are called Tier 1 and many others who don't qualify then make it to Tier 2, Tier 3, and so on. Imagine a student who couldn't make it to a Tier 1 college. He is now branded for life by the corporate system. So what will he do—he will now gun for a MBA from a Tier 1 college. This thinking of breaking the structure is deep-rooted from the pecking order explained above. It has devastating effect on a student's psychology and confidence.

This pecking order is everywhere. It is visible in how students choose jobs as well. The job that pays the highest is the first in the pecking order and it largely depends on the words 'sunshine sector'. Today, I think in the engineering world it is the IT sector. In the MBA world, it is finance and consulting. Again, to clarify, the pecking order has no correlation to whether the choice is right or not so right for the student. But it is a big reason for students to make choices anyway. It is perceived that those who do get placed in the top companies in the pecking order are the most successful from the batch. I personally don't agree with this but that's another matter altogether and not the purpose of this book.

The hierarchical orders stems from our age old Varna systems as well. As a culture, we do look up to certain things and it is not easy to change that. In my opinion, it is all about the mindset of an individual. If you want to live like a global citizen then you have no choice but to break this thinking. But I do understand that this comes with maturity and for a student of 17 years it is very difficult to ignore a pecking order and go against it.

## *Fear of failure*

This is the 'mother' of all problems for the younger generation. As a society, we have a huge fear of failure. We seldom encourage risk taking behaviour. To give simple examples, a family will invest majority of their savings in fixed deposits in a state owned bank or a public provident fund as it is a safer bet. Gold is another safe bet. Stock market is considerable very risky. Mutual funds come somewhere in between. Now let's understand why everyone doesn't want to go for the high risk, high return stock market. That's because from our childhood, we have been taught to take the safer road—fixed deposits and gold. There are 'guaranteed' returns for these roads. The returns may be lower than inflation, but that doesn't matter.

A child or student of today is taught to be a conformist and choose a road which is well-trodden and hence safe. When I told my parents (in class 11$^{th}$) that I want to be a chef, there was outrage at home. Our middle class systems revolted simply because of the fear of failure and 'what if...' thoughts. There was a classmate of mine who chose Arts as a subject—the only one of us to do so. And in my times, arts were something that only girls chose. He became a social outcast from that moment. Today he is teaching English in a university; and his example is always taken as 'learn, or you will end up like him' by parents in our circles. The fear of failure is always around. It is combined with all the other six factors mentioned above.

1. Why doesn't a student take up a job in an unknown company working on a new lubricant for motors? It's because first, he thinks that a job in that sector is very dirty as compared to working in an air conditioned office

of say, a bank; secondly the oil and gas sector is a sunset sector; and lastly, he is afraid of failure and being stuck.

2. Why doesn't a student go for a course in music? Again, due to lack of social acceptance and fear of failure of finding a good job afterwards. You don't see an advertisement in the job portals with the title 'Wanted: Music Manager for an MNC', do you?

You name a problem, and you can usually find an answer in 'fear of failure'. Some other fears that students face are the fear of getting rejected, losing identity, having physical or mental pain, making commitments, making wrong choices, not being in control and lastly, fear of getting reprimanded.

# Been There Done That

The next few chapters of the book are stories of ten top alumni of IIM Bangalore. Read how they made their choices when they were your age, how they swam through the waters and what they did to reach where they are today. Each chapter also represents an industry sector with information on the kind of work students might expect in them.

# Arun Balakrishnan PGP '76

*Director HPCL–Mittal Energy Ltd*

*Former Chairman HPCL India*

As I began writing this book and crystallized the plan for choosing alumni for the chapters, the first person who came to my mind was Arun Balakrishnan. He is an alumnus of the first batch of students from IIM Bangalore and is also a Distinguished Alumni of the institute. I met him for the first time in 2009. He was the chairman of Hindustan Petroleum Corporation Limited (HPCL) at that time. The human mind can get very prejudiced by titles and designations. So when I got an invite from the batch to join their reunion party and also to meet him, I was slightly intimidated. But my first handshake with him shattered my bias and fears. He is a very affectionate and approachable person who can welcome everyone with his sincere smile and humble attitude. He and his batchmates made me feel comfortable in that gathering. I was probably the youngest in that room—could have passed for somebody's son. But I was treated like an equal which is the nicest and most special quality of the entire PGP '76 batch. I felt the same warmth and affection when I met Arun in 2012 at the iconic and lively Koshy's café to interview him for this book. He retired from HPCL in 2010 but shows no sign of stopping and is now an independent director on the boards of many top companies of the country.

## The Formative Years

Arun did his schooling from St Michaels School in Cannanore (now Kannur) in Kerala. He enjoyed the culture of the institution that encouraged sports, physical activities along with good academics. The school had many visitors and priests from all around the world who valued and encouraged reading and writing books beyond the ones compulsory at school. His mother inculcated in him the habit of reading before going to bed that helped him immensely and which he continues till now. In those days, the first decision of choosing subjects and streams came in 11th and he chose Mathematics. His logic was quite simple. Since his dad was a doctor, he had a slightly rebellious approach to Biology and hence Math was the obvious choice. In those days, information was not that easily available but his elder brother was a big influence and through him and his friends, he heard about various engineering colleges like RECs, IITs etc. But he couldn't write the exams due to issues of travel and dates and chose to enter the Government College of Engineering in Kerala. In those days, chemical engineering was considered to be a prestigious stream and he took the advice of his seniors and opted for that. Halfway through the course, he felt that he had made the wrong choice and asked his professors if he could switch or drop out from the college. They advised him to continue and finish. By that time, his elder brother had entered IIM Calcutta and he also decided to join one of the IIMs for his MBA. He wrote the exam for Bangalore and in 1974 became a student of the first batch of the institute. At IIMB, Arun was very active in both academics and extra curriculars. He was the editor of the first student magazine called Hocus.

In 1976, as the placement season at IIMB began, Arun waited with excitement as this would be the first taste of corporate life for him as he hadn't worked after his engineering. In those days, only public sector companies visited the campus and Arun was hoping to get through HMT which was the dream company for most of his batch. Unfortunately, he was not shortlisted for HMT. He tasted his first failure but resolved to learn from it and move on. He then got calls from ICICI and HPCL. Both were good in their respective fields of banking and oil and gas. He decided to join HPCL as it had a more multinational culture because of its history with Esso and Caltex. In hindsight, he feels his ability to decide quickly was a great blessing for his career as he moved forward. This is something he does till today—take decisions quickly without spending too much time over-analyzing options.

Things were not given to him on a platter at HPCL. In those days, the management trainee cadre was very new and Arun had to struggle to make his presence felt. He persisted and spent the first three years learning the ropes of the trade and preparing for his first project. His first big break came in 1980 when he was sent to be in-charge of setting up an LPG bottling plant in Bangalore. It was a gruelling and challenging project which required Arun to get down to the basics of the engineering in setting up the plant, to getting his team, to identifying the contractors and making the plant to deliver as per schedule. In two and a half years, the plant rolled out its cylinders into the market and Arun was recognized as a person who could deliver. He applied the basic lessons of management that he studied at IIM Bangalore, understood the importance of people in getting work done and this became his strength later on. He points out that one of the most important phases in the career of any student of today is the first few years of starting in a job. He feels that many students just leave for other opportunities without taking the efforts and getting their hands dirty. Arun says that one of his favourite books *Outliers*, also stresses on this point and quotes, 'There is no self-made man. One must understand that one has to first be a part of a system, learn it, deliver, and then make it better with time. For anything to work, one must spend upwards of at least 10,000 hours on it. That's approximately 14 months.' However, anecdotal evidence suggests that a majority of students leave their first jobs within six months. It is such a colossal waste of opportunity that could have been realized if they had persisted for more time and proved their worth.

## The Rising Star

In 1982, Arun was asked to move to Calcutta and manage the operations in the East. He welcomed the challenge, took it on with excitement and moved with family to a city which he had never seen before. He faced numerous challenges there—cultural shock, language barriers, tough unions, 'chalta-hai' attitude of the staff, and languishing sales, to name a few. This was where he saw his opportunity to learn and make a difference. In the five years he spent in this assignment, Calcutta region became #2 in sales overall for HPCL and his colleagues, customers, and stakeholders saw his sincerity and fairness for everyone. The management of HPCL recognized the leadership qualities in Arun and he moved on to taking more challenging assignments.

'Never say no to any new opportunity just because it's in a different city,' says Arun. He points out that students nowadays tend to select only those cities where they want to settle for a lifetime and this restricts career progression. One must have an open attitude to go see the world, learn new cultures, and be open to taking on any challenge. He feels that a person who is seen to be a flexible but firm person gets more opportunities to grow as compared to those who are picky and choosy.

By mid-nineties, Arun steadily grew up the ranks. In 1994, he was asked to represent HPCL in the Oil Coordination

Committee (OCC) as the country began liberalization and privatization of the oil and gas sector. This needed Arun to move to a role which was more policy oriented, required him to liaison with the Oil Ministry and the various departments of government bureaucracy. It also was something that needed him to completely disconnect with HPCL to avoid a conflict and run the risk of losing the 20 year credibility he had created for himself in that company. But again, he took it as a challenge and an opportunity. In the five years that he was with OCC, India saw its biggest economic growth stories happen. Arun was a key member driving the positive growth in the oil and gas sector of the country. He enjoyed excellent relationships with the ministry, various companies in downstream petroleum who wanted new projects in refining, and LPG plants and pipelines. The impact of all that work made every family of the country benefit from these policies. Many of us won't know how difficult it was to get a gas cylinder in those days. It is down to the new economic policies and the work OCC did to increase capacity and jobs that we can now order gas on mobile phones. Arun's work again got him massive success and he finished that assignment only to be called back at HCPL for bigger and better things.

After OCC, Arun became GM for Lubes and launched new products for HPCL and made it a very recognizable brand in the country. Again, he says that he had no background in Lubes—he didn't even know much about this space until he took on the assignment. Lubes are used in machines as a lubricant in a variety of applications and HPCL was not leading the market at that time. Sales were languishing every month. There were a lot of foreign brands and they dominated the market which was highly fragmented. Arun says that this was when he applied the Marketing 101and Chemical Engineering 101 to his job. He and his team first did a simple analysis of various products and price points in the lubes segment. They then visited hundreds of workshops and cities to see how they were used, who were the customers, how they buy it etc. They figured that the end customer was a simple mechanic who was probably not even educated and very price conscious without diluting quality. This later helped them in positioning and branding this product. He and his colleagues setup a small research and development (R&D) team to configure a completely new product that could be manufactured at the price point they had identified. It wasn't easy but Arun felt it was worth giving a shot.

'I like to do things which are new, have never been tried before and require hard work. In return, I get to learn so much.' With this philosophy, Arun and his team created a Lube that became the highest selling Lube in HPCL's history. It was called 'Laal Ghoda'. The punch line was 'ghode ki taakat, chane ka bhaav' translated to 'strong but at an affordable price'—incorporating the learning from their research regarding price sensitivity. They made the product available in sachets to allow customers to get more choices on the quantity and it also helped them reach economies of scale. The label on the packaging was mostly pictures showing the product applications which helped the uneducated customer to connect to it and hit a home run. In 18 months, sales catapulted from 0 to 20,000 kilo letres a year which is a record and had the largest brand recall in its segment as compared to its competitors. Laal Ghoda continues to be the topmost selling product from the HPCL stable.

Arun says that no education is useless. Though he never really applied his chemical engineering in the first decade of his career, it came in handy at some phase of his life. The same goes for any other branch of studies. He is very certain that a student may study something and do a job that is totally different. He is sure that education is an important foundation on which careers are built and will be useful someday. A job will give all necessary and adequate training to every student anyway. So he feels that students should not do too much analysis paralysis on choices in the early years. They should simply decide which sector they broadly want to work in and choose accordingly. He feels that knowledge is important and not degrees. Skills are important and not certificates. And students tend to focus more on what is not important.

In 2007, thirty-one years after joining as a rookie management trainee, Arun became the chairman of HPCL. He continued in HPCL despite observing his other batchmates and friends hopping jobs in 'lucrative sunrise industries', earning a fraction of what many of his age and credentials were getting. He does not regret it one bit. He thoroughly enjoyed being in the same company and feels that he got more opportunities to

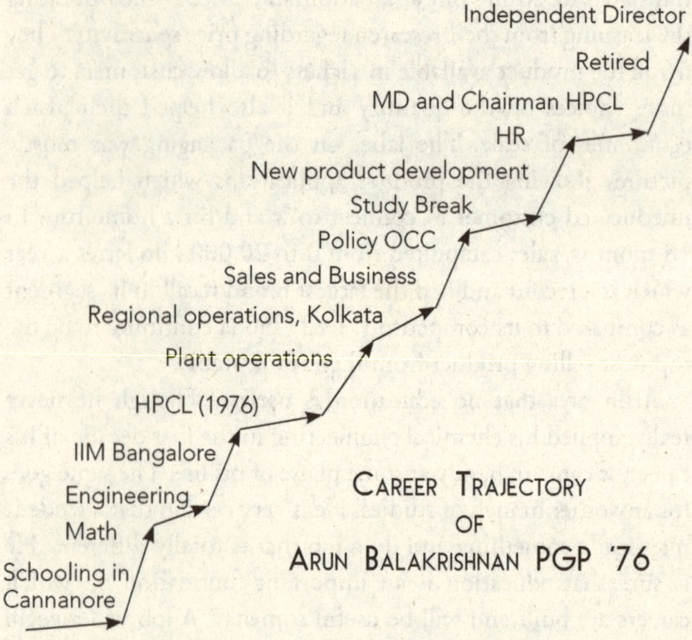


CAREER TRAJECTORY OF ARUN BALAKRISHNAN PGP '76

do all kinds of things within one company than anybody else he knows. He stands tall as an example that hard work and patience do pay—may be slowly but steadily.

## Key Messages to Students

As we enjoyed our second coffee at Koshy's, which was now bustling with patrons from all over, I asked him what his career advice would be to students.

1. **Take up any opportunity that comes your way. Avoid analysis paralysis** – Arun feels that this is the most important message to students who have too many choices and hence too much confusion in front of them. He also feels that social pressure is a big reason for students to make career choices which could be unproductive. He gives an example from his own career choice at HPCL to support this message. In the early 2000, when Arun was at the peak of his career after launching Laal Ghoda, setting new plants, and managing business units, he was asked to head the HR department of HPCL. From my own experience of social pressures in the corporate world—if I was VP of sales of Mumbai and West, my entry to the HR department would either be treated as a demotion or a definite suicide on career path to the CEO job. I don't mean that HR jobs are lowly. But this is the social pressure that I would feel if I were asked to take up the HR head role (as Director of HR) after heading sales.

   However, Arun didn't let that thought come in his mind at all. He again looked at it as a brilliant opportunity to make a difference. In those days, the HR department at HPCL was more of an IR department—handling industrial relations and not human resources. Arun had read the strategic importance of people for an organization and how the world's best companies invested heavily in their own people. Being known as a people's person, he thought he could drive the same philosophy at HPCL and make it even better for generations to come. He felt that this could also be a key differentiator between HPCL and all its competitors in India. Without batting an eyelid, he took up that assignment. Arun's biggest task was to first make the HR department useful to the needs of HPCL employees. Till then, employees probably didn't know or cared for an HR department at all.

Arun first analysed how the employees contact the HR department. He found out that most employees called up the HR desk to book a holiday in one of the many HPCL guest houses throughout the country. This was a big perk in the company and every two years, the employees availed LTA (Leave Travel Assistance—a government scheme that allows employees to avail tax benefits on vacations every once in two years) and took their families to the best places of the country where they could also enjoy a 5 star stay at the guest house at really no extra cost. So when an employee tried reaching this person at HR desk to book a guest house for them, either he would find the line busy or if they would get through, the person would answer in a very curt manner, 'Guest house is full'. To be fair, this person was not necessarily being unhelpful on purpose. If you had a job answering people who wanted to know, 'When is the guest house of Darjeeling free?' twenty-five times a day, you would be curt too. This is where Arun saw an opportunity. He called his IT team and asked them to make a simple software that could show all the guest house availability online for every employee with a simple click of the button from their browsers. Something like an online railway reservation system, but on a smaller scale. In just three months, the pilot was ready. The employees were thrilled to see information accessible anytime and with fairness and the HR department suddenly became the darling of every employee. Arun then rolled out many employee friendly policies that made the HR department a very integral and strategic part of the organization. He feels that one edge he had for the chairman's position was his ability to work in every department—from sales to administration to HR.

2. **Think out-of-the-box** – Arun suggests that every student should try and think differently and find new ways of solving a problem. It may not always be wise to take things head on, especially when the opponent is stronger and better organized. It's very easy to follow the norm and do what has been done before. One should explore newer ways of solving problems related to decision-making. He illustrated this with a problem he faced with the union in the Mumbai Lube Blending Facility. This was an old factory where the union often indulged in 'restrictive practices'. Workers would demand overtime even in normal day shifts. Production was paralysed if the management didn't agree to giving them overtime or other unreasonable demands. The workers used these tactics because they knew that if they stopped production, sales and business would be greatly impacted at HPCL. Arun initially tried to solve the problem the conventional way—which was by calling for a meeting with the union, negotiating a better way, penalizing the problem children etc. Nothing worked. He and his team figured out a completely out-of-the-box way to solve the problem. They decided to open a brand new factory with the best of modern technologies, fully automated shop

floors which required lesser but highly qualified workers as a way to send a message to the Mumbai factory. In less than two years, a factory with state-of-the-art equipment was created and it was fully automated. The machines were so modern that one could put a carpet on the shop floor and it would not be spoiled by any grease or a wayward drop of oil. The supply chain was efficient and the moment the product was ready, it was shipped off to retail stores.

Once the operations became smooth, Arun hired three buses, brought all the workers of the Mumbai factory to this one, and gave them a tour of the new workplace. The workers saw a great factory which made more profits and knew they were in trouble because they realized they could go on a lockout with no major impact on HPCL. Sometimes out-of-the-box thinking can do wonders. It is slow and may take lot of effort, but it is worth it. The same thinking should be applied to careers. Find a new way of doing things and make that your career. It could be an existing sector with a very mature system. But you can always find a newer, better way of tackling challenges.

3. **Take a break every once in few years** – One of the best phases of Arun's memory at HPCL was when he was given a six month study leave to go to the UK. He was in his 40s, had worked and proved himself, and lapped up these months to learn new things, experience a new place, immerse in a new culture, explore, and generally charge his batteries. He feels that in hindsight, this gave a massive boost to his career when he came back—fully rejuvenated and ready for more. In those six months, he completely switched off and focussed on himself and his family. He learnt how the UK companies were

building new business models, observed the oil and gas industry trends in bringing newer technology that would impact the country and the overall trend of the world as becoming a global village. 'Take a break every few years—be it on a study, or to pursue wanderlust. Just switch off, recharge yourself for few months. Your mind and body need nourishment too,' says Arun.

## Myths Shattered

1. **I must change my company to get better opportunities** – Arun is the best example of how one doesn't need to change companies to go higher up the ranks. This is a very common misconception of students. Many of them change jobs within 1-2 years thinking that it opens up more opportunities. That's a myth. Within HPCL, Arun got a chance to do every possible dream job one can ever hope for. Many a times, he felt the pinch when he saw his peers who switched to the sunrise industry buying new cars or a bigger flats, or going on glamorous vacations with the joining bonus offered by the new company. 'But it all evens out with time,' says Arun. One should stick around for at least five years to know the sector and be productive. It's a personal choice at the end of the day.
2. **Always choose a 'sunrise sector'** – Arun feels that students must look at a sector from a 25-30 year horizon. Few years ago, when there were rumours that the oil and gas reserves would deplete by 2020, many students had written off the oil and gas sector as a 'sunset' sector. But that is not the case. With the recent discovery of Shale gas reserves and the boom in technology to do better exploration and distribution, the oil and gas industry is here to stay. It may

not be a sunrise industry which helps people make billions in a few years, but it definitely is no sunset industry either. Energy creation, sustainability, and efficiency are new buzz words the world is beginning to use and this sector still has enough to carry on for next 2-3 decades at least.

3. **I might stagnate faster as this is an old sector and there is not much to learn** – Arun feels that students should not worry about this too much. There are smart people in the oil and gas sector. They won't let this sector go into the sunset and will find new ways to keep it attractive and lucrative from commercial and learning perspective. Technologies become outdated and every person should continue to learn new skills and technologies to stay current. Same is the case with any sector. Few years ago, Java was hot in the IT sector. Now it is mobile applications and android/IOS. So something new will keep coming up and if someone misses one train, not to worry. The next one will come soon. Stagnation will happen only when the candidate is not keen to learn. If you remember the 'Survival of the fittest' theory by Darwin, similar theory applies in the corporate world and any sector. 'Innovate or perish' is the mantra now. Oil and gas is nowhere close to the 'P' of perish as there are huge innovations happening.

### Opportunities in Public Sector Units (PSU)

There are several different definitions of a great place to work, depending on the different people that you ask for suggestions. But one thing remains common apart from a good pay package—the great place of work has a management you can trust. People working there have pride in their jobs and the employees work and get better as a team. PSU Jobs are often taken as a recession-proofed career!

The PSUs are classified as Maharatna (Coal India, IOCL, NTPC, ONGC, SAIL, BHEL, GAIL), Navaratna (BEL, BPCL, HAL, HPCL, MTNL, Nalco, OIL, etc), and Miniratna (Airport Authority of India, BEML, ITDC, NHPC, MRPL, IRCTC, Hindustan Copper, Goa Shipyard, HMT, NFDC, etc). They offer jobs in all categories and one can stay tuned to opportunities in jobs advertised on their websites or on the employment gazette.

## Malavika Harita PGP '82

*CEO Saatchi & Saatchi Focus Network India*

MALAVIKA HARITA IS AN ALUMNA from the PGP '82 batch of IIM Bangalore. She is currently the CEO of Saatchi and Saatchi Focus Bangalore and walks, lives, and breathes advertising. Her dad worked in the army, her mom was an acclaimed Bharatnatyam dancer. She was the elder one of the two children in the family and learnt the role of being responsible very early in her life. The family was very academically inclined, there were books everywhere in the house and the parents encouraged both children to follow their hearts. There was art and sports liberally sprinkled as well to counter the academics. Malavika was a bright student, excelled in the class, and was very interested in Science. In 10th grade, she decided to take up Math as she really was good at numbers and found the subject fascinating. She didn't like Zoology or Botany which eliminated the Medicine route for her career. When the time came to choose between engineering or BSc, she chose the latter because she didn't see herself fitting the labs and doing forging, smithing, carpentry etc.

Her dad had retired from the Army and had setup a small packaging unit, after a stint at Kirloskars. In 1978, he took out his bike to do some work one day but met with a fatal accident. Malavika was just 19 and being the eldest of the siblings, she realized that she has to take charge of the family business and be the man of the house. She decided that she will not let her younger brother worry about the business and other household issues and let him study and pursue his academic interests. She continued her BSc in PCM (Physics, Chemistry, Mathematics) on the side. Her love for Math came in very handy when she was running the company. She did all the accounts by herself. Her mother also stepped in and they both ran this business for about 15 years. After her BSc, she wanted to study further. She thought her love for Math, accounts etc. would ideally be the right reason for her to apply for a CA (Chartered Accountancy). But when she was doing the articleship, she found the overall environment too dreary and uninspiring for her to continue further. Leaving Bangalore for doing something else was not an option as she had to take care of her mom, and the business. Luckily two of her close friends from college were already studying in IIM Bangalore, which was a new and upcoming college. They often told Malavika about the subjects they studied and the amount of fun they had. So she decided to apply and in 1980, got selected for the PGP programme at IIM Bangalore.

Malavika recalls those two years as the best in her student life. She decided to be a day-scholar as she had a company and home to manage as well. She was able to do justice to both easily, though. Since she was actually running a business on the side, she could relate very well and learn from her management lessons in class. Her through knowledge in Math and Accounts proved to be another blessing as she breezed through the finance subjects. She stumbled into the world of marketing as a discipline. She loved the subject, the concepts of understanding customers, marketing campaigns, the marketing communications, and advertising. She was one of the most popular students of the batch. She owned a typewriter; in those days, to submit reports, one had to go to a DTP Centre to get a report typed or stand in a queue for a computer which had a word processor and a printer. So she became the default report writer of her group. She still cherishes all her friends and batchmates—a lot of them are now entrepreneurs, CEOs, grandparents, and so on. The subject she enjoyed the most in those two years was advertising. While she was good at Math and Accounts, she was bored of them and decided to not go in that direction when applying for jobs in IIMB. Somewhere, the academic in her also nudged her to think about a PhD but for that, she would have had to again leave Bangalore which she firmly decided not to. Even till today, she doesn't regret this one bit. She feels that sometimes constraints are good guiding principles in life. Instead of feeling bad that the constraints don't let you move, accept them and find space with what you are left with without diluting quality. She feels that she has achieved more in Bangalore than what she could have outside. When the time came to apply for jobs from campus, she applied to Madura Coats in the marketing department but they had a policy of not hiring women at that time. Finally, she decided to apply to HMT and got selected in their marketing department and she joined HMT in the latter half of 1982.

As the marketing manager in HMT, her job required her to manage the advertising and sales promotion for HMT watches. She was given a budget of ₹4 crore—a great responsibility in those days. She loved handling the agencies who worked with HMT, creating the advertising campaigns, and had wonderful bosses who supported and trusted her. This was the time that Quartz watches were just about to be introduced in India. She loved her work and the kind of exposure she got. Her mother gave her full support by managing the packaging business by herself. Like a blink of an eyelid, six years passed. She had gotten married during that time. Somewhere, work became duller and she wasn't enjoying it as much as she ought to. Her bosses had left for other jobs or assignments, the company had grown and had become slower and bureaucratic, and she was expecting her first child. So she decided to take things slow for a bit and focus on motherhood. In hindsight, she now realizes that the moment she feels bored of a job or feels that she isn't learning anything new; she knows it's time to make some changes.

Motherhood was the perfect project she opted for instead of another job. Her son was born in 1988 and she enjoyed being a full time mommy. During those years, she took up interior decoration as a hobby. She read about the subject while her little baby was asleep and experimented with her own house. Her friends and family loved her style and taste. So she decided to take up the interior design hobby a little seriously and started a small outfit. It gave her the much needed dose of doing something professionally but at her convenience. She could take her son along when she was doing projects. Slowly, her name spread and before she knew it, she had setup a very successful company that catered to select clients through word-of-mouth. She applied her knowledge of numbers and design, acquired a capable team of carpenters and designers, and made good profits too. She continued to help her mom with the packaging business as well. But very soon, she realized that she was becoming a glorified carpenter and was sure that she wouldn't enjoy it beyond a point. Again, the moment she felt that she was not learning anything new, she strove to make a change.

She weighed her options. She decided to go back to her first love—advertising and joined Mudra and later Sistas. Sistas was later acquired by Saatchi & Saatchi and this was the beginning of a long love affair with this company which continues till date. A key lesson for youngsters, that Malavika points out here, is to maintain relations with batchmates and colleagues. Personal networks are like SIP mutual funds. They grow but one must keep investing in them. Her comeback to the industry was because of her relationships and networks that she had maintained over the years.

She started her stint at Saatchi & Saatchi as an associate account director for a client. Her work got recognized and she moved up the ranks very fast. Soon she was heading the Bangalore branch of Saatchi & Saatchi and increased the operations and sales of the branch by adding new clients and building new offerings. By 1997, she felt the urge of changing her environment and getting a booster shot of learning. She didn't want a change in her job. She really enjoyed Saatchi & Saatchi, the people, and how it was shaping up. But she craved something totally different. So she found out about the Gurukul Chevening Scholarships (given to professionals under 40) and got selected. Her joy knew no bounds. She was going to be a student again—and this time at London School of Economics, studying globalization under Lord Meghnad Desai himself. The scholarship took care of travel, stay, and incidentals. The classes were exactly the change she desired and the best part was that her peer group of 12 fellow scholars were from all sections of the society of India—writers, reamers, industrialists; but they were merely students in that class. She thoroughly enjoyed being a nobody along with them. They also got a chance to meet the Queen of England. They travelled across UK, bonded with each other, and felt thoroughly rejuvenated.

She started Saatchi & Saatchi Direct on her return from England to cater to non mass media focussed clients like Bosch and Coats.

Malavika's plan was a resounding success. The business grew manifold and she realized that she was like an entrepreneur at Saatchi & Saatchi but with a monthly pay check. For her, it was having the best of both worlds. The headquarters loved her idea and encouraged her to continue on this road. Her next big step was to take this idea to the technology companies of Bangalore which was being touted as the silicon valley of India. Companies like HP, 247Customer, etc became her clients and she helped them in building their image for hiring talent in India, making their products and services easily understood by their customers, and helped them build their online marketing footprint. Saatchi & Saatchi Focus in India is not a run-off-the-mill advertising company. The Saatchi & Saatchi Focus Network is a knowledge based communications agency which caters to the specialised communication requirements of companies in the B2B, IT and Talent spaces.

In 2010 she started Saatchi & Saatchi Health to cater to the requirements of Pharma companies, hospitals and medical equipment suppliers. She is now experimenting on how to use digital technology to get the message across. The impact is much more and the same collateral can be sent to the doctor's phone where it will be utilized better when he/she needs it.

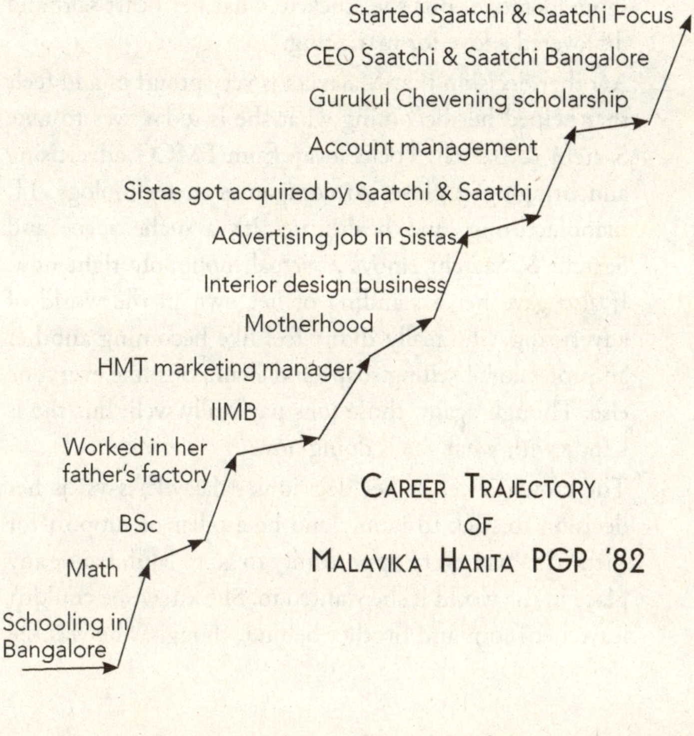


Career Trajectory of Malavika Harita PGP '82

## Choices to the Top

1. The best career choice Malavika feels she made was to opt out of CA and finance. As a child she had a love for Math and numbers. This grew to accounts and using this skill in her family business. But very soon she realized that it was too dull and decided to stay away from it as her full time focus. At that time, when she was 19, it was not an easy decision. Many students prefer to stick to what they know best as they are in their comfort zone and hesitate to venture out to new areas. But she moved to IIMB—something that she had not much idea about besides her friends' opinions—a new institute in those days. Even in IIMB, she could have opted for finance and taken up a job in a bank which would have been financially more lucrative. But she stuck to what her heart said and discovered a love for marketing.
2. Another decision that Malavika is very proud of and feels that helped her becoming what she is today was to take Saatchi & Saatchi Focus away from FMCG advertising and bringing it closer to companies in technology, IT, manufacturing, and healthcare. It's a niche space and Saatchi & Saatchi enjoys a virtual monopoly right now. It also gave her a standing of her own in the world of advertising. She really didn't feel like becoming another ad professional selling soaps and shampoos like everyone else. Though again, those jobs pay really well; but she is happy with what she is doing now.
3. The crown jewel of her decisions, Malavika says, is her decision to stick to family and be a pillar of support for them. She had every opportunity to go to Mumbai or any place in the world if she wanted to. She knew she couldn't leave her mom and brother behind, though. She was the

elder sibling and she donned the role of the head of the family after her father's death without any hesitation. She doesn't feel that she sacrificed anything. Instead, she got the best of both worlds—to stay in Bangalore with her mom and carve a magnificent career for herself in the wonderful city.

## Key Messages to Students

1. **Make sure that you are the best rat in the rat race** – There is no space for mediocrity in this world. It's a very competitive market and the good old Darwinian concept that only the fittest survive holds true in careers too. Malavika advises, have a very competitive mindset and aim to win. If you have decided to enter the corporate world which is called the rat race, be the best rat and stay ahead of the pack.
2. **Pay off your educational loans and move on** – Malavika understands that a big difference between her time and the students of today are the educational loans. In her time, she and her entire batch almost got the education for free. Not today. She is aware that the students graduate with huge debt on their shoulders. They take decisions based on the monetary value of their jobs more than the kind of work. She feels that it is okay for a student to take up the highest paying job even if it isn't the ideal choice. Once you are into the job, remember the advice given above. Be the best, prove yourself, and make sure that even if the job is dreary and boring, you do it with your best foot forward. It will teach you lessons which will help you in the future. Make sure you close on your loan and move on. A decision based on debt will always have short-term results. Think long term and don't miss the woods for the trees.

3. **Make your boss redundant in six months** – Work hard and prove that you are capable to doing more, in fact, take up things from his plate and start doing them. There is a fine line between sincere efforts and flattery of which Malavika warns. If done with earnestness and sincerity, the results are wonderful. If your boss starts to give you his work, it means that you are on the right track. She has always benefitted from this philosophy. In every job, she would prove that she could do her boss's work too. She didn't make them feel threatened. Instead they loved that their work was onw being done by someone younger and they had time for other things. This has two benefits—one, you win the confidence of your bosses and two, you get promoted too.
4. **Treat internships very seriously** – Last but not the least, Malavika thinks students should take their internships very seriously. It's a wonderful way to learn about a company, explore options, build relations, and experiment whether you really like the sector/company or not. Most students today take up internships to adorn their CVs but don't relate to the company or the work. They don't even attempt to network and meet people other than their own friends and other fellow interns. She feels that this time can be utilized to the maximum potential by them to explore people and the sector and get paid as well.

CAREER OPPORTUNITIES IN THE ADVERTISING SECTOR

An advertising company has three broad areas for careers—each of them require a totally different skill and interests from the person who wishes to work here.

- Research – where the ad agencies conduct and study markets, consumer behaviours, brand recalls, product positions, competitive analysis, and basically 'study' the environment. Research professionals are often well versed in mathematical modeling, project design, and communications methodology.
- Creative – The creative branch of an advertising company is charged with conceptualizing client messages in an artistic form. This conceptualization can span all kinds of media, ranging from print to audio and television. Creative departments take expert steps to tailor client messages to the particular audience they are trying to influence or persuade. Creative professionals within advertising are experts in various art disciplines ranging from traditional artistic disciplines like creative writing, screen writing, and drawing to more advanced desktop publishing techniques.
- Account management – Professionals in the account management realm of advertising are responsible for maintaining open lines of communication between the client and the agency. Account management employees stay abreast of current campaigns to make sure they are running smoothly, on budget and within deadline. Account managers must always be open to the desires of current clients, while simultaneously tracking potential new business leads. Advertising account professionals have a stronghold in business communication, sales, project management, and networking.

Some sources for students to know more about this sector is to browse the 'Brand Equity' supplement of Economic Times, or websites like AgencyFaqs.com. There are also professional bodies like Adclubs, global awards like Effies (the Oscar of advertising world) given to those who work in this sector. Globally, it is a very well-known sector with rich clusters in the fashion capitals of the world. In India, most of the ad companies are in Mumbai and Delhi with satellite/local offices in Bangalore, Chennai etc. There are many entrepreneurs in this space—thanks to the ever evolving media technologies and consumer preferences. These trends have given rise to niche careers like photography, ad movie making, graphics design, signage, and consulting. The online and social media have brought in careers like Campaign manager for Facebook, LinkedIN using platforms like Google, InMobi etc. Overall, advertising is the only sector that is able to balance both the creative and rational side of life under one roof. Some famous ad agencies are O&M, JWT, Mudra, FCB Ulka, Rediffusion DY & R, Mckann Erickson, RK Swamy BBDO, Grey worldwide, Leo Burnett, and Contract.

# N. Ravi PGP '82

## *Former Secretary Ministry of External Affairs*

As a child, one of my dreams was to become a diplomat for India in some country of the world. I don't know how this thought got seeded in my mind. Most children of my age would typically rattle 'I want to be a fighter pilot' when asked what they want to do when they grow up. Then, a neighbour enlightened me that if I wanted to become a diplomat, I would have to clear the civil services and join the Indian Foreign Services to fulfil my dream. As I grew up, I drifted miles away from that dream. A big reason was that I found the UPSC exam extremely intimidating and chose to take a comparatively easier path.

Thankfully, there are alumni like N. Ravi from the 1982 batch who are brave enough to get into the foreign services and inspire people like me. A very soft spoken and warm human being, he retired from the post of Secretary in the Ministry of External Affairs in December 2009 and is now a Senior Fellow at the Centre for Public Policy in IIM Bangalore. I was always puzzled about the logic behind an IFS officer doing an MBA. However, N. Ravi is no regular alumnus. He walks his own road. Born and brought up in Delhi, Ravi feels that his career was shaped by his environment. His father had worked in the Government of India and since childhood, his teachers and school mates talked about IAS/ICS and he was enamoured with this path as his career. He also nurtured a childhood dream of being a rocket scientist or a pilot—anything that could take him in the realm of space. In 1965, a year ahead of finishing high school, Alexei Leonov, the Russian astronaut had just completed the space walk and Ravi too, dreamt of a career connected to space travel or space science. In 1966, when he had to make his first career choice between choosing subjects, he chose Chemistry as he felt that he could do something in the area of rocket fuels. NASA USA or the Indian Air Force was his dream destination.

To the latter end of the year, he had filled up the NDA entrance examination form, and stood 3rd in rank. He got called for an interview for a place in the Air Force as that was the only choice he had marked in his NDA form. He cleared the interview and appeared for the week long medical examination. All parameters were clear, and on the last day, the medical officer, asked Ravi to take off his shoes, wet his feet, and walk around the room. Ravi obediently followed the instructions. He got the shock of his life when he was told that he had flat feet and was not qualified medically to join any of the wings in the air force.

The officer explained the reason for this. One of the requirements during training is to jump off from a height to the ground—to simulate parachute jumping. Here the role of the arch of the feet is vital. The moment the feet touch the ground after the fall, the arches absorb the shock of the impact. Those with arched feet can sustain that impact. However, those with flat feet may suffer fractures of the legs and back. In Ravi's case, observing the imprints of his wet feet, the medical officer remarked that the first jump could be Ravi's last! And so, one of Ravi's dreams shattered.

He took a few days to emerge from this episode. His parents counseled him on the road ahead—either to get into engineering or continue in the science stream. He couldn't make it to the engineering college and chose to do BSc in Chemistry from

Delhi University, because of his interest in rocket fuels. His dad bolstered him,'You tried your best. If things don't work out, learn and move on. Don't get bogged down by failures.' He completed his BSc with honours and later did his MSc in Chemistry. Furthering his interest in space, Ravi took up astronomy as his hobby. Even today, he enjoys spending hours gazing at the skies in the night with his telescope, occasionally glimpsing the International Space Station when it traverses the sky over Bangalore.

As he explained, his career decision was more a factor of his environment. After completing MSc, Ravi had to choose between writing the IAS exam or GRE. The environment in Delhi University was clearly thumpingwith 'taking a shot at the IAS' and landing a top job with the government. Even as a child, living in a government colony, he had interacted with many who had written the civil services exam and joined the services. At the time, GRE was a very expensive proposition which didn't really appeal to him. By now, his dream of space had turned into a hobby and he was quite happy with that arrangement. Again, his ability to 'move on' helped him to stay grounded tremendously.

To keep him busy, his dad referred him to a friend who ran a business of making accessories for X-Ray clinics like the X-Ray viewer, heaters, and stencils. (In those days, once the X-Ray was taken, one had to manually write the name of the patient with a stencil and then dry the film after development using a heater. For viewing, one had to put the sheet on a viewer which was actually a box with a Perspex screen and a tube-light for illumination at the back.) Ravi's job was to assemble the units and he learnt the importance of patience and manual work. He enjoyed doing this as it also helped him concentrate on his studies and gave him few hours of diversion. He realized that he would rather be in civil services than be a businessman working on X-Ray accessories. He decided to prepare whole heartedly for the UPSC exam. He appeared in the exam in November 1972, cleared the interview in April 1973, and joined the Indian Foreign Service, in July 1973, as a Probationer.

The first two years are spent in training both through academics and practical aspects. Every candidate is sent to various departments across India to learn the different facets of the job. It's like a drill that everyone has to go through. Unlike many of his age, who were in the corporate sector, Ravi knew that he would now retire as a government servant. It was a very relaxing and liberating feeling which allowed him to enjoy his training even more. In 1975, he was given his first posting in Belgrade, in former Yugoslavia.

He loved the experience of living in another country, learning their language, culture, and working in the embassy. He met people from various countries and thoroughly enjoyed learning various aspects of diplomacy and what really makes up the Foreign Service. He spent a little over two years there and returned to India. The desk bound job at the headquarters was too routine and somewhat limited in variety. This urged Ravi to see if any avenue for professional advancement existed outside the system. He was waiting for his next assignment and had some time on his hands when he heard about the IIMs from his school friends and also found out that he could take study leave from his ministry. His intention to do an MBA was to give him more tools and a broader perspective to serve the country better in the realm of the Foreign Service, which dealt with Commerce and Economics. India was a growing economy and he realized a need to understand the Indian and the global economy, business dynamics to do his job better. A two year programme would give him just the right grounding, he felt. In hindsight, this was one of the best decisions of his career.

Till then, before his MBA, he was doing what he saw around him and what was told to him. But now, he started taking his own decisions. He had a very supportive boss as well who recommended his application. There were the naysayers around as well. Many of them cautioned him that this could be his exit from the ministry and that he would lose plum opportunities. Also, some at the ministry feared that he might resign and go to the corporate world once the MBA was finished. But he was undeterred. He informed the ministry that he had no intention of quitting and signed up a bond to allay their fears. The ministry approved his study leave. In 1980, Ravi came to IIM Bangalore and joined the PGP programme—the only one in the class who had come on a study leave and probably the eldest in the batch as well. The two years at IIM Bangalore gave him a wonderful platform to learn various subjects of management. He found the experience extremely enriching. He did not apply for placements and returned back to the ministry.

Soon after his return, he was posted to Tokyo as First Secretary (Economic and Commercial). The two year MBA programme paid off. In 1984, Ravi had the opportunity of shepherding a delegation of twenty chief executives of public sector organizations from India, through the heart of the Japanese economy and industry. The visitors were being escorted by the legendary professor of marketing, late Mr Labdhi Bhandari of IIM Ahemadabad. At the time, he could clearly see that there was hardly any difference in the engineering competence of the Indians and the Japanese. However the system in Japan was geared towards manufacturing, technology, and exports while that of India was oriented towards development, capital acquisition, and investment attraction. Japan as a country was way ahead of its times and Ravi's knowledge of business, economics, and politics came in handy in building good relations with the Japanese government and business enterprises. This in turn resulted in beneficial initiatives from the ministry to bridge the awareness gaps in Indian industry which was just beginning to become aware and appreciative, of the new world order. In 1985, Ravi hosted a top Indian delegation of 15 industrialists and ministers from India to Tokyo. He recalls that in a single bus, the who 's who of Indian business houses were present and he was taking them around to meetings with the Japanese ministers and industrialists. This episode gave him the renewed confidence that he could now work with governments and business enterprises with ease. The MBA programme gave him the skills and tools to understand nuances of the Japanese economy and aspects like marketing, sales, international business, human resources etc in Japan. His proficiency in the Japanese language also helped immensely in bridging the culture of the two groups.

He returned to India in 1985 and wanted to expand his skill set in a different arena. Having acquired a good foundation in diplomacy and additionally armed with management skills, Ravi requested the ministry to give him an economics-oriented assignment that could enhance his skills further. In response, he was posted as director in the Foreign Trade Division of the Department of Economic Affairs in the Ministry of Finance. The geographic contours of his job covered Eastern Europe, an area familiar to him. On another facet, the job dealt with the financing of Foreign Trade, management of Foreign Exchange budgets of the Ministries of Defence, Shipping etc. The tenure in the Ministry of Finance saw the transformation of the Soviet Union through the process of Perestroika and Glasnost—the consequences of which changed the world completely. He dug his nails into the world of commerce and finance in this role—the plate comprised negotiating credit agreements for infrastructure projects in the power and coal sector; deferred payment facilities for large scale equipment purchase; financing of trade plans; and a host of other financing-oriented work at the international level. In these tasks he was able to use softwares for doing NPV analysis which only reinforced his belief that he had taken the right decision to join IIM in 1980. In a sense, his dream of using some management techniques directly in his work was realized.

After successfully completing the stint in the Foreign Trade Division in the Finance Ministry, he was posted to Bhutan in 1989 as Counsellor and Deputy Chief of Mission at the Embassy of India in Bhutan. This was when he really started to enjoy his career which was blooming. Every three years, he did something new. And this time was even better. In 1989, the role of the Indian government was central in helping most development aspects of Bhutan. Power was one such area where, with the help of Indian government, the first hydel power plant at Chukha was established. As the official in charge, and overseeing existing and identifying new projects, Ravi feels that this was the best assignment he did, as it directly impacted the society and lives of people in Bhutan. India completely bootstrapped the Chukha plant (338 MW) operations with the help of talent and skills from India in the phase 1 of the project. During phase 2, they gave the technology and knowhow to the Bhutanese so that they could carry the growth forward in their own way. This was very satisfying to Ravi as he was able to see a nation grow and know that he contributed something in that regard—bringing two societies together—in his own small way. Bhutan is one of the most beautiful places on earth. He enjoyed his stay in exotic forests, and came face to face with a herd of elephants 10 metres away! He learnt to respect nature and the wealth it contained.

This was the most fulfilling time of his career. He and his team did a lot of work in Bhutan at the ground level as he learnt and saw how two societies could come together for a common purpose with the governments playing a crucial role in shaping the future of a country. He understood the value of politics between nations and how it was like a job that somebody would do—similar to finance, marketing, human resources, economics, strategy etc.

As he looks back, he sees that he has worked on economic and commercial projects, combined with political work while working in different societies and countries—a very rich variety of exposure that no other job could probably give. He feels that one of the reasons he got this rich variety was his ability to ask for what he wanted. He asked for leave to do an MBA, he got it. He asked the ministry for the finance ministry job and got it. Then he asked for the Bhutan job and he got that too. So the feeling that students have today about civil services being drab and boring work, festooned with corruption and bad ministers as bosses, is more of a perception than a reality. It is a very rewarding career just like any other corporate career, in some ways even better.

After finishing this assignment in Bhutan in 1992, he was posted to Tokyo as Deputy Ambassador, because of his knowledge about Japan and his proficiency in the Japanese language. At the time, Japan was in a political flux. The political parties were in a state of turmoil and for the first time in four decades the political power was slipping from the Liberal Democratic Party, Japan's own GOP! He remarked that during his first stint in Tokyo, he had seen two prime ministers preside over Japan. In the latter period, i.e., 1992 to 1996, there were as many as five! This was the consequence of two major scandals—the Recruit Cosmos Share Scandal and the Sagawa Kyubin Scandals.'[1]

---

[1] The Recruit scandal, was an insider trading and corruption scandal that forced many prominent Japanese politicians to resign in 1988.

The most interesting part of this phase was that since he was fluent in the language, he was able to relate and connect to the Japanese society quickly. Between 1992 and 1996, he worked on many business proposals between the Indian and Japanese governments. He also witnessed the gradual decline of the Japanese economy.

Ravi feels that every student must pick up one extra language each from India and the International array, besides Hindi/local language/English. It really helps the student appreciate and learn more about the world. Above all, it definitely helps while looking for new jobs. Most students, he feels, just focus on money and pick up degrees and skills that they think will get them fatter pay cheques. He says that money will eventually come. However, the formative years can be better utilized in learning different things besides amassing degrees and also working harder and delivering whatever you are asked to do. He says that students should make sure that they choose something that makes them learn at one level and enjoy at another.

He returned back to India in 1996 and joined the Ministry of External Affairs for a year. He was itching to do something different, when an opening emerged in the Ministry of

---

The scandal knocked out the Prime Minister Takeshita and his government. Takeshita's political secretary, who had received money on his boss' behalf, hanged himself. His suicide note read: 'Behind the scenes of this peaceful democracy are the same bloody struggles to the deal that were waged time after time by medieval warlords.' In the early nineties, after months of rumours and speculation, the Sagawa Kyubin scandal involving the governing Liberal Democratic Party broke with police raids of the offices of a large trucking company that reportedly funneled hundreds of millions of dollars to top politicians and organized crime.

Commerce. With the approval of his superiors he joined the Ministry of Commerce. Again, his MBA helped tremendously. His first assignment in this position was to organize and service a dialogue meeting of industrialists and exporters with late Prime Minister Gujral. Some 40 business leaders including chairmen of top companies, exporters, and bankers attended the meeting that went on for about 4 hours at the Vigyan Bhawan, New Delhi. The delegation had come prepared and raised lot of issues and concerns on the Exim policy of the country that made life hard for them. Ravi realized that many of these problems were actually very simple to resolve, if only these were addressed sectorally.

The issues ranged from very trivial things like a minor change to a form, to a big change in policy to moderate levels of taxation and duties to bring in more revenue. The Prime Minister announced the setting up of the first ever Export Promotion Board of India, under the chairmanship of the Cabinet Secretary and Ravi was appointed as Member Secretary. He did this for two years and developed a great insight into the public private partnerships of the country. He felt rewarded and this board became a game changer for the public private relationships. In hindsight, he now feels that although the job was not very challenging, it was very fulfilling for him personally. He became a channel for the private sector to work with the government. The industrialists and the government acknowledged his management style and his ability to get people together and show results.

Many of the interactions with industrialists revealed that low productivity in India was not because the Indian labour force was poor or that we didn't have skills. The issue was that Indian industrialists had to spend enormous amounts of time meeting the regulatory inspectors. Many a times these inspectors would just land up unannounced in the factories and stall production.

The whole day would be wasted. This had a negative impact on the production and hence the output and thereby exports. Mostly, it was an archaic formality being adhered to because no one suggested a way out. Mutual discussions often yielded simplification of procedures and significant saving in time. Many a sector benefited from these interactions at the newly formed export promotion board.

Again, here is a great learning that Ravi gives for students. Ravi feels that instead of fighting and criticizing the issue—typically delays (harassment in this example)—bring in a constructive dialogue to address the problem and find a creative solution.

No official likes to be called inefficient or dishonest. He is merely doing his job as per the policy. So if the policy and the mindset can be changed for everyone's benefit, why not approach that as the solution and resolve all issues? The moment we make it personal and start focussing on the people and not the issue, everything is lost. As Benjamin Franklin famously said, 'Well done is better than well said.' Talking about a project won't get it completed. We all know people who constantly talk about the things they are going to do but rarely ever take that first step. Taking action and seeing the task through to completion is the only way to get the job done.

After two years in the Ministry of Commerce, Ravi was asked to shift to Moscow in 1999 as the Deputy Ambassador. He was quite happy in the Ministry of Commerce and the routine that had been established. The proposed move to Moscow was quite a bolt from the blue. He was not prepared but he decided to take it up as he was sure that something good would come out of it. As mentioned earlier in the chapter, his philosophy was to take whatever came his way in his stride, and do a good job, rather than spend time analysing and saying no. In a sense, the career exposure to Russia/Soviet Union was coming full circle. Having worked in the MEA (1977–80) on the East Europe desk and again in the Ministry of Finance (1986–89), Ravi was now preparing to work in a 'new' Russia where the Communists represented just another political party! It was a country that had seen a huge change in its politics and society. Putin was the new sheriff in town and they were taking control of state's resources back from the oligarchs and bringing stability in the country which had seen extreme civil turbulence for nearly a decade after the collapse of USSR. His fluency in Russian also helped him understand the social changes in Russia during that decade. The period he spent in Moscow reaffirmed to him the age old saying: 'Boast not thyself of tomorrow; for thou knowest not what a day may bring' [Proverb 27:1].

In 2002, he moved to Munich and setup the first resident Consulate General of India. He remembers that he and his team actually bought furniture, chose the colours of the drapes themselves, and enjoyed building the office with their own hands, as it were. Those days were rather relaxed, he adds. While they were at it, one morning, a lady walked in for a visa to visit the Ramana Ashram in Tiruvannamalai in Tamil Nadu. Elated that a Consulate had opened in her home town she applied for the visa even though the Consulate had not officially started functioning. Her tickets were already booked; all she needed was a visa. Ravi and his team were waiting for approvals from the Indian authorities. However, this lady was quite determined and said, 'You will find a way!' She waited all morning as Ravi and his team made special efforts to get the necessary approvals for the issue of the visa. By afternoon, Ravi got a go-ahead signal to issue the visa. It was like a magical moment. Ravi had not expected that the approvals would come so fast and easy. This lady who had been quite hopeful said, 'I knew I would get a visa.' He felt some kind of karmic connection and thanked the lady for being the first person to get a visa issued from the Consulate General of India in Munich.

In early 2004, he was appointed Ambassador of India to Vietnam. By now he was well known in diplomatic circles and was respected for his rich exposure across many cultures and particularly for the diversity of portfolios he had handled. He started getting invited to business schools to give lectures on international affairs, political economy, and other subjects. He loved this new experience. He has a great regard for the people of Vietnam. Despite all odds, here was a country that had demonstrated progress in a very short span. They reduced poverty, scaled up production, invested in education, invited the world to invest in them, and through sheer determination, hard work and a grit to survive, bounced back on the international radar. He often takes their examples in the classes on how societies collectively come together after a steep descent and lift themselves towards a common goal. In this stint, he was instrumental in setting up a cross country computerized communication and training network in six Vietnamese universities with the help of Government of India and thereby came closer to the educational environment. This was the peak of his career. Many other projects for human resource development were put in the pipeline for implementation in subsequent years during his three year posting in Vietnam.

Now the only thing left in front of him was to ascend to the top post: become secretary in the Ministry of External Affairs. In 2006, he was posted back to Delhi as Secretary in the MEA. To explain; the MEA is headed by the Minister and has two Ministers of State to assist him. The political triumvirate is assisted by three secretaries with the Foreign Secretary being the first among the equals. This official triumvirate runs the MEA and Ravi was one of the trio now. His career had come full circle—he joined as a Probationer in1973 and was one of the top officials in 2006. In this role, he handled India's relations with more than 70 countries of the world (each country has an Embassy of India, with an Ambassador that reported to him). Overall he was like a CEO with 70 divisions reporting to him—almost half the world.

Ravi feels that it has been a very fulfilling journey. In December 2009, he retired from the Foreign Service and joined as a senior fellow at IIM Bangalore, in November 2010. In October 2012, he brought in a delegation of students from Myanmar for a 10 day programme at IIM Bangalore and is now

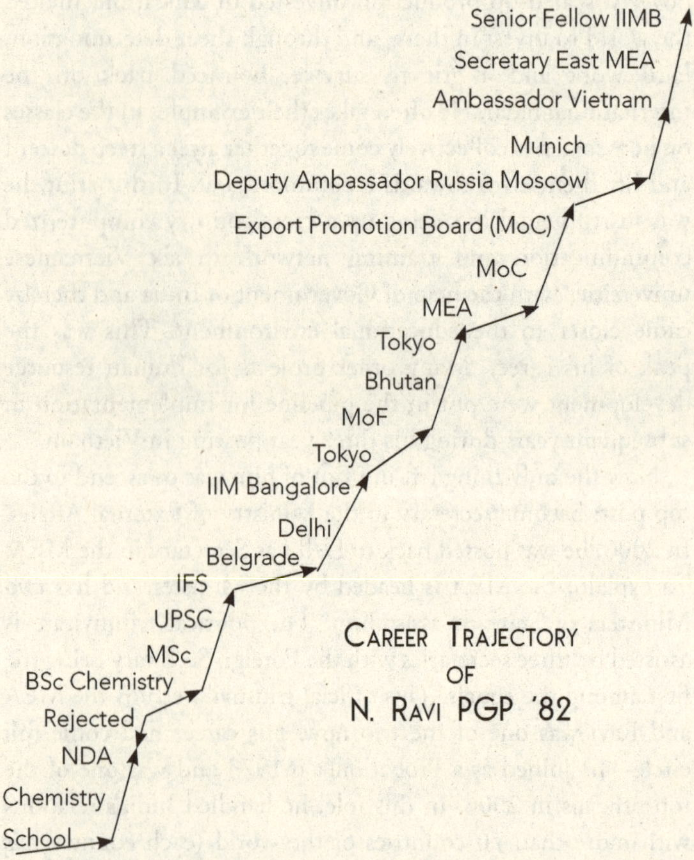


CAREER TRAJECTORY OF N. RAVI PGP '82

working on more such programmes between ASEAN countries and India. He spends a lot of time teaching and meeting young minds who are going to shape the future of this country and the world.

## Choices to the Top

1. **If you miss the train, just find the next available one and move on** – The most important choice that Ravi took in his formative years was to choose the civil services over GRE. He knew he couldn't afford going to US and realigned his childhood dream of working on rocket fuels. Most of the time, we revel in our own depression and blame everything around us. It's like being on the station and waiting for your dream train to come. When it does, you are unable to get inside and end up spending your life on that station. Ravi moved on to the next platform and took the next available train.
2. His next best career choice was to move into the Ministry of Commerce where he became the Member Secretary of the Export Promotion Board. It gave him a tremendous visibility into the private sector and helped him bridge their needs through policy changes. He walked the road less travelled. Most of us, if we were in his shoes, would not even dare to move out of the MEA. He decided to because he wanted to learn something new, and he got rewarded immensely in return.
3. In 1999, he was asked to move to Moscow. He really was unprepared and unwilling but he thought it through and consulted his superiors. In hindsight, it was perhaps this posting that catapulted him towards the top job in MEA.

## Key Messages to Students

Learn a new language or acquire a new competence that complements and adds value to your career and helps you learn. All through his career, Ravi kept on acquiring new skills and knowledge. Be it a new language or a totally new course like an MBA programme. He feels that these are the reasons he was able to move up faster and do a richer variety of work as compared to his peers.

If an opportunity comes your way, try and think why you have been chosen. Avoid jumping to a 'Yes' or 'No' immediately. Consult your superiors and mentors as well. But try and take it up, work hard, and demonstrate your skills.

Manage your boss well. He or she is the boss because they have done something better than what you can do. One can never choose bosses or parents. In the case of civil servants, the bosses are ministers who are politicians. Ravi feels that they are no different than managers of a corporate. They have a job to do. Though the environment is different from a corporate organization, they also want results, and if you can be their go-to guy and show results, they will support you and give you all resources you need to make things happen. They are extremely smart people too. Many have started their career in grassroots politics—as social workers, then gone on to be a corporator, MP, and so on. Their greatest asset is people management. They have a firm grip on their constituencies and are very business savvy. They also have their ear to the ground and are quite clued in. Learn to manage with your bosses and focus on your job. The philosophy of the Gita—do your work without worrying about the fruits of your labour (they will follow, in any case) is quite apt for civil services too.

### Opportunities in the Civil Services

Just like an organization has various departments and units, similarly, India is also a large organization which is managed by the Central and State governments. The government is then broken down into smaller department called ministries and need officers to work for them. These officers are recruited through the UPSC exams, made to go through rigorous training programmes, and then based on qualifications, interests and merit, placed in different ministries. Being an IAS officer is a job of tremendous responsibility. Some examples of ministries where such officers would work are Ministry of Defence, Railways, Finance, External Affairs, Home Affairs, Agriculture, Power, Corporate Affairs etc. There are at least 100 such ministries both at central and state level. Then there are many independent bodies like the RBI, SEBI, Planning Commission which recruit IAS officers. Police (IPS) and Forest (IFS) are also big departments in their own right.

# Bhargav Dasgupta PGP '92

*CEO ICICI Lombard*

Bhargav Dasgupta, from the 1992 batch of IIMB PGP programme, is currently the CEO of ICICI Lombard. He was born in Calcutta to a middle class family with strong values. His father was working as a chartered accountant in a multinational company. He was a good student in school and did quite well in studies. In his school, there was an option to study Biology along with Math and Physics in the Class 10th-12th Science stream. He opted to study both Science and Math, and then choose after the 12th exam on what he should decide to study further. His mind was firm on either engineering or medicine because his social group, friends of the family around him, and the seniors from school had been more inclined towards these options. He did quite well at both engineering and medical exams and had the option of choosing either one. But he tilted more towards engineering because to establish oneself as a doctor, it took 15 years or more. There is a lot of academic rigour involved to become a doctor—MBBS, MD, DM etc. Engineering required only 4-5 years to get a good job. Since his father worked in the private sector, he had enough examples of how engineers became more successful much faster as compared to doctors. So he decided to move forward on the engineering track.

He chose to do mechanical engineering because of his interest and passion for cars—the design, engine, speed, and moving parts that go in the making of a car. In those days, computers and electronics were not very popular. Many colleges had very few seats for these new branches. And he felt that mechanical was a more popular stream which also provides a variety of choices to work after graduation. At college, Bhargav enjoyed designing, constructing of mechanical projects—like designing and manufacturing a reciprocating pump from scratch. He loved the forging and fabricating labs and was excited by shop floors, using tools and giving shape to a working, moving machine that would do something meaningful. It was here at college that one day; he saw the annual report of Tata Motors. He read from the first page till the last, felt connected and related to their work, values and vision. And that was when he decided that this was his dream job from campus. He persisted, waited for Telco to come for campus placements, and got selected. In 1988, he graduated with flying colours and joined Telco in Jamshedpur.

There was a huge mismatch between the dream of what he thought he would do and what he actually did at Telco. The year book that he read in college depicted engineers working on shop floor and designing and making trucks. And what he actually did was far from it. He was put in maintenance department and he found himself oiling and lubricating parts or fixing problems in the machines. Maybe it was the wrong expectation set by the limited information he had from the yearbook that time, or maybe he was destined to be elsewhere, at that time it didn't matter really. What mattered was that he was young and these were formative years. He knew that he had to make a change because he was not enjoying his work at all. The options in front of him were quite simple; either apply for another job in some other company—maybe Maruti, or Ashok Leyland—or take up another educational degree as his parents were advising him and find better opportunities beyond engineering. He was clear that GRE or MTech was something that he didn't want to do. He was also very clear that he would not leave India. He decided to write the CAT and get a management education. The two year stint at Telco also gave him good ground to realize opportunities in management and the dynamics of a corporate setting. He was convinced that the MBA programme was the best option available to him. He had a natural propensity to grasp financials as it was a topic commonly discussed at home. All roads pointed to the CAT and the MBA route—he joined IIM Bangalore PGP programme in 1990.

Naturally, in the first year, he gravitated more towards finance subjects. He got high grades in the batch and was a consistent performer. He also had figured out that the options out of IIMB were either in banking/finance or marketing. Given his strong interest in finance subjects, he learned that a career in finance meant banks like Citibank, ICICI, and Bank of America etc. He luckily got a summer placement in Bank of America (BankAM). They liked his work and gave him a verbal offer to join them after his course got over. But somehow, that offer never translated into a concrete one. Bhargav didn't let that worry him. He did some research on companies and was attracted to ICICI as it had a great reputation and name. He had seniors working in ICICI and they were doing some amazing work evaluating companies, their business plans and then giving industrial loans. ICICI at that time was not a retail bank as it is today—it specialized in project finance and didn't have a swanky office in BKC in Mumbai. By now, he had figured out from his disillusionment at Telco that he wouldn't let looks, appearances, and salary of a job factor in making a decision. He decided that he would make a choice on the quality of the work. Though Citibank was an American MNC and paid a lot more, he knew that the quality of work at ICICI was much better than Citibank or BankAM. ICICI became his dream job and he really worked hard to qualify for it. When you really want something, the whole world conspires to make it happen. He was shortlisted and got selected in ICICI from campus. He has used the same philosophy of making career decisions ever since—focussing on the quality of work. Money, designations, and titles follow.

In 1992, he joined ICICI as a young management trainee. He was put in a team but there were some organizational changes planned and he was asked to await his specific role and portfolio for the first few months. But Bhargav was patient. In the long run, this quality of being patient has helped his career a lot.

Patience paid off and he got his first assignment. His first assignment was to evaluate a particular project proposed by a large company and give a summary to his boss on whether ICICI should fund that project or not. He was given a big fat document which had details of the company, the project they wanted money for, the overall industry they were operating in, the trends of this industry, the technology used, the value chain—it was like all of the 96 credits of IIMB rolled into one mammoth report. It was a few thousand pages. He was expected to digest this mammoth and burp out a crisp flash report—about 4 pages of summary and a pithy recommendation. This was the first lesson at ICICI—hard work and attention to detail. He took a good one week to finish this assignment and submitted his 4 page flash report to the credit committee of ICICI. His personal assessment was—risky. This report was accepted by the credit committee and they rejected the proposal of this company. Bhargav was just 25 years and he felt empowered. He felt like he could make a difference because ICICI took his work seriously, trusted his judgement and this strengthened his resolve to continue working for the company. He loved the kind of work he did every day and was fortunate to have supportive bosses. During the first 4-5 years, the exposure was phenomenal. He spent a lot of time in understanding business plans and overall business trends of the world. India was changing rapidly because of the liberalization and Bhargav was at the right place at the right time. There was a tremendous amount of action happening and ICICI was right in the middle of the growth story of a country, financing its mega projects and helping the nation grow.

He continued to work in the group that financed projects related to engineering, non-ferrous metals, paper, rubber etc. By 1995, he saw most of his peers leaving ICICI and being lapped up by the broking firms and banks that had opened up. He, however, decided to hang on. ICICI now had new management structure as well—Mr K.V. Kamath was now the CEO who brought new dynamism and put the company on a growth path. He put national focus on infrastructure and oil and gas projects. Bhargav got the opportunity to join this group. He was one of the seniors in the oil and gas division and was asked to take few of the junior members under his wing. This was his first brush with managing people. The team did quite well and became one of the largest financing groups within ICICI.

In 1999, the e-commerce bug bit ICICI. The company realized that internet would change the way businesses present themselves to customers. There was talk about the dot-com companies offering various exciting solutions in the Silicon Valley. Hotmail and Yahoo were buzzwords. The ICICI top management wanted to e-enable their business and also fund e-businesses. Bhargav was asked to join that group as a second-in-command. It was a completely new area of work and very risky. But Bhargav took it as a challenge and dived into the projects. Unfortunately, the dot-com bubble burst within six months of his joining this group; and everything collapsed in the economy. In that little time, ICICI had already invested in few dot-com companies and it was decided that they will stay to protect the investments and exit from some of them which didn't have a chance to succeed. In this process, he learnt a lot about Internet and technology which helped him in his future roles at the bank. He worked hard to merge things back to the main businesses of the bank, protect whatever was invested in the e-commerce projects, and minimize the losses.

In 2001, Bhargav joined the CEO office in strategic planning and technology. His stint in e-commerce was a big boon here. He first studied the futuristic trends in technology sector and prepared a report on where ICICI needed to invest for the future and diversify beyond its existing businesses in India. He spent a little less than an year on this assignment which was actually the foundation of ICICI's international operations. A key part of this plan was that ICICI should create an international footprint. The plan was presented to the board and he was asked to take charge of ICICI's international operations in 2002. It was like throwing a man who couldn't swim into sea, without a life jacket. Bhargav and his team were hard core finance people who had always worked in India. Things like retail banking, international customers, etc were new topics for them. They narrowed down five or six countries and started operations of ICICI in these countries from a scratch. These were USA, UK, Canada, UAE, and Singapore. These places had huge populations of Indian residents, called NRIs (Non Resident Indians), who were either settled there or had come to work for a short period. They all would send money back to their parents or families in India. This was the market they decided to address. Up till now, an NRI who was working in a foreign country, say Canada, would use a Western Union Bank or an equivalent and transfer money back to India to his family. So the way it worked was—Scenario 1—the NRI would give money to the Western Union Office in his country of residence and get a secret code. He would call home and ask his family to go to the nearest WU outlet in their city, use the secret code and get cash over the counter and then deposit the cash to their personal bank account. WU would charge a huge chunk as commission—up to $40 per transaction. Scenario 2 would be that an NRI would send a bank cheque to his family in India and it would take anywhere between 3-4 weeks for it to get encashed by his family in their local bank.

Bhargav and his team envisioned a technological platform that could deliver the same service and directly deliver the money to the bank account in India. The first solution not only transferred the money directly to the bank in India, saving time and the trip to the outlet, but charged just $5—facilitating huge saving per transaction for NRIs and a massive opportunity for ICICI. In the second scenario, ICICI would partner with the local bank of the country, became an intermediary and get the cheques cleared in 4-5 days—as compared to 3-4 weeks. They then expanded the scope and started providing complete NRI Banking Services in India, built local branches in UK, Canada, etc to service their local needs and even got local Canadians and English to start banking with them. Apart from the retail business, they built a large corporate and investment banking business serving the Indian corporates as they started globalising. They had a three year breakeven plan but outperformed it in just a year, spread from 6 to 15 countries and began contributing significantly to the ICICI collective revenues by 2005. That's a huge impact to ICICI in just 4 years. All this was through technology and thinking out of the box that Bhargav feels he learnt during this e-commerce experience. While the e-commerce investments paid back handsomely 5-6 years later, at the time it had appeared to be a financial disaster. Even then, it sowed the seeds to a larger project that bore fruit a few years later. There is a Harvard case study on ICICI's international expansion plan. This is a lesson Bhargav wants the students also to remember—being a part of a failed project doesn't mean that your career has failed too. The learnings from that project will be useful someday. One must focus on doing the work and avoid thinking about the success/failure aspect.

The stint in ICICI international skyrocketed Bhargav's career. In October, 2006 he was promoted to the position of executive director on the board of ICICI Prudential Life Insurance Company Limited. Life Insurance was a new line of business that ICICI had ventured into a few years back. The country and its culture are very different for an insurance business. In other countries, most adults look at insurance as a must-do aspect of their life and think of death/accident etc as a risk for which one must safeguard themselves. But in India, these topics are a taboo. To give a simple example, the Indian customer understands a bank account and a savings account very well because he knows the value of savings and investments in fixed deposits and schemes that help his money grow. But if you approach this customer and say that 'you might die or might get hit by a truck', it will not help him realize the value of insurance and he will perceive you as a threat and a bad omen. There were huge costs incurred by the insurance company to acquire customers, promote their brand and be one of the 10 choices of policies in the market. LIC was a big name already. Bhargav was asked to scale the business and added new lines of business. He also strengthened the distribution by focusing on the basics and increased market share. Overall, the two and a half years that he spent in ICICI Prudential helped him develop capabilities of running a large scale retail distribution business in urban and rural India that he didn't have before.

Bhargav was promoted to be the CEO of ICICI Lombard General Insurance Company in May, 2009. The General Insurance Industry was going through a difficult phase at that time. Apart from the impact of the 2008 crisis, the industry was reeling from the impact of detariffication (freeing of prices) in 2007-08.

Some competitors dropped prices by as much as 90 percent. Prior to 2008, the focus was on scale and growth. But by 2009, Bhargav and his team put entire focus to transform from scale to managing what they had, managing risks and managing their customers. They carved out a new five year plan and involved the whole company to give inputs for it. It created a lot of positive energy in the company. The employees felt involved in the company's change-management programme. Overall, it was a big success and ICICI Lombard is doing well because of strategic thinking, focussing on quality of business, not on scale like other competitors did, and involving the entire company to contribute towards the vision.

Working in a new industry brings a lot of new opportunities to learn new things. Bhargav says that the insurance industry has a very unique working model. There are a lot of steps to be taken for one policy to be given out and each step comes with a cost. Regardless of whether the policy is for ₹500 or for ₹5 crore, the steps are similar and so are the costs. One has to contact the customer, get some forms filled up for the Know Your Customer (KYC) process, then send everything to the processing unit for the policy to be issued, and then courier the same back to the customer. This requires a lot of manpower, technology, and co-ordination. At the same time, margins are razor thin and everything has to be managed in that tight margin so that service is delivered to the customer in an affordable manner. So the entire operation of a company has to be designed on an extremely low cost delivery model. Nevertheless, there is scope for innovation. Here's one example of how Bhargav and his team at ICICI Lombard innovated the operation for the rural markets. Given the stringent processes of KYC and the operating costs to acquire a customer, the rural market posed a serious problem. First the ticket size of an insurance policy was quite low—some as low as ₹500. And second, if the same steps are applied here, then the courier of the KYC documents to the head office and then sending them back to customer added a lot of cost and complexity—there are many places which don't even have courier service. So they came up with a brilliant idea. They sent their agents with a printer and empowered them to collect all documents, and issue a policy right there using the printer. That threw up another interesting problem through. Many places had no electricity. The laptops could work on battery but the printers couldn't. Bhargav always knew that technology could really be used to bring innovation. So he took the suggestion of a team member to use the energy from the bike's battery to power the printer when needed. They had a vendor design a small unit that could plug the battery interface of the bike to the printer and it worked. It brought costs down significantly and made their brand a lot stronger in the rural areas.

As the CEO of ICICI Lombard, Bhargav explains that he has a very execution-focussed job that requires him to do two other things. The first is people management and he now realizes that subjects like influencing skills, communication skills are more important than just accounts, finance and strategy. He feels that the job of a manager/leader/CEO is to help his team do their job better. He has to stop sitting in an ivory tower and has to spend more time with his ear to the ground where his employees and customers are. The other part a CEO has to do is manage stakeholders like members of the board, government, thought leaders and build his credibility to influence them for the overall goal of the organization. Bhargav says that students of today should really focus on subjects like HR, Organizational Behaviour, influencing and communication skills along with other subjects. He argues that the world is getting so competitive that one can easily get smart candidates who are armed with good education from good institutes. What is missing in most of them is their ability to be good managers and good humans at the same time. Degrees and titles don't matter beyond a point. It's personal credibility and a bank balance of emotional intelligence that matters to get the job done.

The second important thing Bhargav does as a CEO is focus on execution and delivery. A CEO has to manage all the employees of the company and the stakeholders like the customers, board, shareholders etc. So execution is of extreme importance. While having a strategic view is important but if the results don't show, the market moves on. So a laser focus on the day-to-day operations, pulse on what the market is saying or doing, and a complete connect with the team is necessary. Bhargav feels that typical human nature is to move onto the next big thing because it is exciting and new. But a CEO can't afford to do that all the time. Some people want to just keep doing new things—without bothering to finish the project on their plate. They should give a project at least few years and see it through. Even if the project is a disaster, make sure that you do your bit that is expected from you. Short term thinking may get them a better paying job but very soon, the market figures

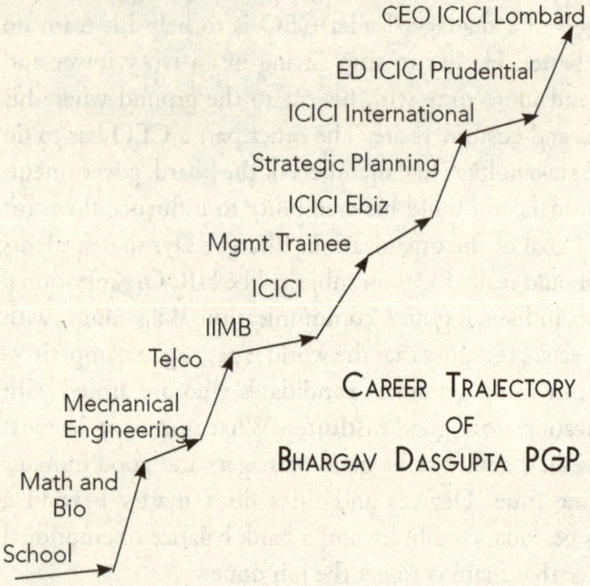


Career Trajectory of Bhargav Dasgupta PGP '92

out that you haven't delivered much and moves on to somebody who can get the work done.

## Choices to the Top

1. **Moving out of oil and gas and into e-commerce** – Bhargav feels that one of the riskiest but most rewarding decisions he took was to move from the oil and gas group in ICICI to e-commerce. He had no experience in the sector but he felt that he had to explore it. Even his colleagues had discouraged him; and when the dot-com bust happened, everyone expected him to leave. He stood fast though, made sure he protected ICICI's interest and also used the learning from technology in other sectors of the company. He was hugely rewarded for sticking to his guns, confirming his belief in having a long-term view and focus on the work. In the same decision, he also regrets one thing. When he was in the e-commerce group, they made a huge investment in a portal which was like Yahoo. It was a hot topic in the VC world in Silicon Valley and they decided to follow the trend and invest. It bombed. He learnt an invaluable lesson—never take decisions based on lastest trends and flavour of the day. One should stick to their core strengths.
2. **Plunging into the international markets** – His second best decision was to explore the international markets for ICICI. He had just come out of the e-commerce situation but that didn't deter him. He took it up as a challenge and ICICI international gave significant boost to the company's top and bottom line. It also catapulted him into the top league at the company.
3. **Staying on in ICICI** – Last but not least, Bhargav feels that staying put in ICICI was a good choice. He could

have moved to a better paying job any day. But he valued work, values, and the overall package more than a fancy pay cheque. He enjoyed working at ICICI and felt that there was no need to move. People leave managers not jobs. He had wonderful bosses and hence never felt the need to switch.

## Key Messages to Students

1. **Career is a long term journey** – 'Short cuts are always blind alleys,' says Bhargav. Destination is important but he suggests that a better way to manage your career is to aim for an enriching journey rather than getting quickly to the end. Students must find a road that offers them learning and fun. The short-cuts may look very tempting but many of them are actually dead ends. So watch out for them. Also, one needs patience to build a successful long-term career. A student must spend at least 3-4 years in their formative years on getting their foundations right. What this translates to is—stick to your job, make sure you learn something, and then think of moving on to something new. Patience is key. Any decision taken in a hurry and with impatience will spell disaster in the long run.
2. **Resilience to withstand failures** – In a typical career spanning 35 years, there will be ups and downs. Bhargav believes that failures are the real test of character and that resilience demonstrated during a difficult period is the mark of a true champion. Lots of people, who taste success early in their careers, find it difficult to handle failure and usually take the easy way out by quitting. Those who stay on to work their way up not only earn the respect of others but also benefit from the tremendous learning that

failures provides. So don't run from a problem, fight it out and try to resolve it to the best of your ability.

3. **Never decide career based on monetary compensation** – Bhargav feels that one should never decide careers based on money. He advises that one should decide on a job depending on the quality of work, the scope of learning, and the opportunity it gives. Money will follow.

### Opportunities in Banking and Finance, also called BFSI

BFSI is a mammoth sector. There are jobs in investment banking, merchant banking, banking sales, insurance product specialists, insurance sales, wealth management (financial advisors), banking service, corporate banking, banking operations, insurance operations, foreign exchange, credit analysis, underwriters, actuarial, financial analysis. support functions in any industry would include: legal and compliance, CSR, human resources, IT and more.

Specific job roles include universal bankers, banking product specialists, relationship managers, trade specialists, marketing associates, brand managers, and many more. JP Morgan, Citigroup, HSBC, BNP Paribas, Morgan Stanley, Goldman Sachs, Ernst & Young, PWC, Bank of America, ABN AMRO, Credit Suisse, Deutsche Bank, Barclays, DBS, Franklin Templeton, Nomura, Berkshire Hathaway are some of the top banks of the world.

Some top financial services companies in India include HDFC Group, ICICI, ING Vysya, Karvy, Motilal Oswal, Edelweiss, Canara Bank, SBI, IDBI, Axis Bank, YES Bank, Kotak Mahindra Group, Bank of Baroda, Oriental Bank of Commerce, and LIC.

# Apurva Purohit PGP '89

*CEO MBPL (Radio City)*

Apurva Purohit not only stands out in the CXO club of corporate India, but also as a person who is sensitive to the cause of women in the workplace. She is often quoted as 'Ms Media' of India but it has not been a cakewalk to where she is today. If you look at the gender ratio in the workplace, it is no rocket science to figure that it is heavily skewed towards men. This topic is debated a lot and may not have a unanimous agreement as of today. But in my humble opinion, the fact of the matter is that women face unique challenges in the workplace, and these are set to be overcome as more and more women participate equally today. This chapter focusses on the kind of career choices women can make to stay at par or ahead of the curve. Apurva writes a blog on this topic, too. Not only has she made Radio City as gender equal as possible, she also has a good view on why more women should consider staying career-oriented and hang in there despite all odds.

Apurva is the eldest of three children and had the chance of staying all over India because her dad had a transferable government job. Her mom was a teacher at a school. Apurva learnt to adapt to new situations and strange cities early. Though she was an academically bright student, she didn't have many plans or a clear career path envisioned. She would follow what her parents or seniors advised. Being a girl, her parents didn't really push her into engineering and she didn't want to become a doctor. One of her aunts was an alumna from one of the IIMs. She secretly dreamed of joining an IIM someday.

This secret ambition drove her forward and after class 12th, she applied for BSc in Physics from Stella Marris, Chennai. Her focus was to graduate and aim for entry into an IIM. So it really didn't matter whether she studied Math or Physics in college because her goal lay elsewhere. In the second year, she started preparation and wrote the CAT. She got calls and finally joined IIM Bangalore in 1987.

## The Formative Years

Her first wake-up call to charting her career came when she was getting ready for a summer internship in 1988. In those days, the placement process was not that complicated. She was keen to be in Chennai and one of her seniors advised her to apply to some advertising companies in the city. She wrote to HTA in Chennai who called her for an interview. Just like that, she had an offer to do a summer internship in HTA Chennai. She candidly confesses that it was a total 'fluke' but, in hindsight, feels that it was her destiny that it was bound to happen. She also confesses that she was not a risk taker when it came to making career choices. She wanted to land any internship that was approachable and did not want to go through the placement process which has a fear factor and the risk of being turned down by the recruiters. So she found this low-hanging fruit and she was very happy to have gotten the offer. She thinks that decisions are just a part of the big picture. After every decision comes the long hard road of executing what you signed up for and that's where she felt she wanted to focus. And this has been her mantra—focus on getting things done really well rather than spending too much time in decision making.

Her stint at HTA was wonderful. She got exposure to the world of branding, customer behaviour, advertising, communication, and had wonderful peers and superiors. Everyone was from some IIM or some other prestigious institution of India and she liked to be one amongst them because she learnt a lot from them. Also, she had taken subjects on marketing so that helped her a lot in those two months. This stint also helped her decide that this is the sector she would probably choose for her final placements. It was fun, challenging and the road into this sector was something she was familiar with because of the internship. In 1989, when the time for final placements came, there were only two advertising companies coming to IIMB—HTA and Rediffusion. Apurva's boss from HTA, under whom she had done her internship, was now in Rediffusion—another advertising company. He called her up and asked her if she was interested in joining Rediffusion after her MBA. And Apurva said yes. One, she was happy to just get over this placement dilemma and avoid the fear factors of being told 'no' by other companies, and two, she anyway wanted to be in advertising. This is how relationships and connections come in handy while choosing a career.

The team of Rediffusion was full of IIM alumni and the agency was on a growth path. She got to work on the Colgate account in the client servicing side. She spent about two years learning the ropes of working with big clients, the entire value chain of advertising—media buying, creatives, communication etc. Then she observed that everyone around her was shifting jobs. And she felt the itch to try out a new job. There was absolutely no problem and no reason for her to look out. The Rediff team and her customers at Colgate admired her work. She just wanted to prove to herself that she too could get another opportunity and do better than what she was doing then. She got an opportunity in ULKA and joined them in a similar role of client servicing but for different accounts. The pay was better too.

She got married to Sanjay, a batchmate from IIMB and in 1993, they were expecting their first child. This is where Apurva highlights that women have to strive harder in managing family and career. She decided to give both her work and her family equal priority. Both are equally important to her and she couldn't see herself doing what most other women around her did—taking a break for a year because of the pregnancy, and then coming back. Many of her seniors felt that the break allows better balancing and prioritizing. She felt that she had the capability of doing justice to both equally. She didn't want to risk leaving the job and then returning a year later to find that she had missed opportunities. There was enough evidence around her that it was not easy for a woman to take a break to bring up her kid and come back to things as they were before. She thought that one needed to be mentally strong, create a support system, and manage a baby with work easily. First she requested her mom to help her balance the home part. And then she requested her boss at ULKA to give her a job that didn't involve much travel, and he agreed. She moved out of client servicing to media buying and planning for the agency.

## The Rising Star

This decision of moving to a strategic role with less travel and asking her mom for support turned out to be a wonderful move for her career. Not only was she able to handle both work and home together with equal priority, she also got two rewards. One—a lovely little boy and two, a new career in media planning and buying which was very nascent in India and growing very fast as the broadcasting sector opened up. By 1995, she was setting up Lodestar—the media buying arm of ULKA because it had grown so much that ULKA decided to have a separate company that just focussed on media buying for all sectors of the corporate world. Media buying and planning can be better explained by an example. Let's say Colgate wants to create a campaign for a new toothpaste they are launching. Broadcast and print have so many channels—television with its own different channels, radio, magazines, newspapers etc; so there is an agency that blocks space in these media which is sold to customers who want to place advertisements and reach to their audiences. This job requires lot of planning, strategic thinking, and managing all stakeholders who are across the spectrum. On one side of the spectrum are the corporate customers like HUL, P&G, CP etc. On the other side are the media companies like Star, Zee, Doordarshan, FM, AM, TOI, Hindu, BT etc. The advertising agencies like ULKA, Rediff, HTA etc act as glue for all of them. It is a massive industry and Apurva was one of the very few experts in this league. The decision of not letting go of her career due to her pregnancy and her decision of working harder to manage both equally paid double dividends now.

In 1997, she was presented with another event where she had to decide between career and family. Her husband got a posting to Chennai. Without any hesitation, she knew she had to move with him. Instead of making a hue and cry, she again used her philosophy that both work and family are equally important. Most of her peers, who were women, would typically sacrifice their careers to give importance to family. But she knew that there was a way to manage both equally. She was quite confident about getting a good job in Chennai. Through her personal connections and friendships in the industry, she got an offer to move back to Rediff in Chennai. This way, she lost neither the opportunity of her career nor had to compromise her family time. In Rediff, she got a client servicing role handling Citibank which was really coming up in India. Her stint in Chennai, though, was short. In 1999, her husband was posted to

Mumbai and she moved back to ULKA. One thing Apurva has learned that she'd like to share with students is that an industry is like a family. If one manages the relationships well, getting opportunities is very easy. Leaving a company doesn't mean that you can't come back to it. One should leave on a good note and not burn down any bridges. One never knows when an old bridge can prove very helpful in finding a new path in one's career. The key is to be open about your plans and keeping your bosses in the loop. At the end of the day, Apurva feels that if you have a good track record, the industry is always open to have old employees back. Companies don't waste time and money in training them and an older employee is productive from the first day of joining. Moreover, this person will bring back a wealth of new contacts and experience that can help the company.

In early 2000, Indian broadcasting sector exploded with exponential growth. And for the first time, in her life, Apurva felt that she should make a bold career move. She knew everyone in the sector. She had an exemplary track record. And one of her ex-bosses had joined Zee TV. They needed someone to head their business and bring a professional touch to the organization. The salary was five times what she was getting at ULKA. A part of her—the risk-averse part—told her to stick with advertising. But another part of her nudged her to try something new and exciting. She hadn't done this kind of work so far and it was a totally new sector. There were no seniors she could talk to and gauge the road ahead. It was like standing on a cliff with a vertical drop. She knew she could fly but was not sure if she wanted to jump because where she was, wasn't bad either. Some of her close friends saw her dilemma and advised her to stay put. They said that it's not a very safe sector and that no one survived a year or more. But something inside her told her to take the offer. She was also finding the job in advertising stagnating with nothing new to learn. Plus, the salary package was undeniably attractive. So she decided to leave ULKA and join Zee.

She jumped from the cliff and expected to start flying. But she plummeted. Why? Because the parachute that she thought she had—her ex-boss from ULKA who had offered her to join Zee and work for him, someone whom she'd known for over 10 years, left within a month of her joining Zee. She could see the dizzying fall and the rock bottom clearly. This is where her self-confidence, the years of working as a professional, and the MBA programme helped. She stretched her wings and told herself that she would learn to fly solo. She told herself that this was a challenge and she will find a way to make things work. And this was the best decision of her career. The first few weeks were scary but she pulled on and slowly made her presence felt in Zee. The Zee business was in a downward spiral because of onslaught from new channels and new programmes. She pulled together her team and worked very hard to stall the downward fall. Slowly the things began to improve; customers came back because they saw a leader in Apurva. She learnt how to work in an entrepreneurial setup, establish processes to make things professional, reduced losses, brought in new customers, and slowly things started picking up. She won the confidence of the Zee top brass and the industry and was heralded in her work.

In 2003, she got a call from Times of India, which was setting up their TV Channel Zoom in India, offering the position of COO. This meant again jumping into the operations of a TV channel, working on technical aspects of the sector—the transponders, satellites, laws, regulations, ministries, distribution etc. She felt that it would give her an opportunity to learn the other end of the spectrum really well. So she took up the offer and spent two years there setting up the operations and expanding the business.

By then, she was a top woman CXO material of the industry. The sector was growing and she was at the helm of the affairs. But she felt that she needed to take her career to a new track and move to a more entrepreneurial setup. The Star group had invested in a FM station called Radio City and one of the investors was close friends with Apurva. One day, he just called to ask her if she would like to join as the CEO. Star was exiting the business and she could also invest a little to buy a stake in the company and also be its CEO to take it to new heights. FM was just in its nascent stages and this was probably the riskiest decision she has ever taken in her life. She knew that she had to step down from a very secure position with a hefty pay packet to being an entrepreneur of a smaller setup, smaller team. In 2005, she became the first woman CEO in a sector that was quite new in India and was aptly hailed as 'Ms Media'.

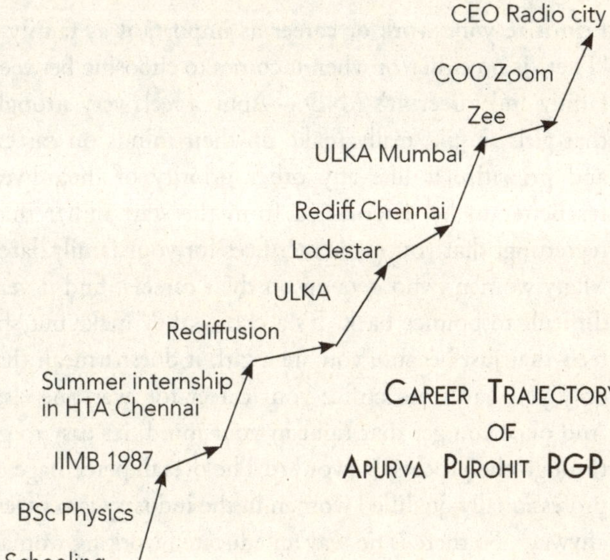


CAREER TRAJECTORY OF APURVA PUROHIT PGP '89

## Key Messages to Students–Especially Girls

1. **No substitute for hard work. 'Don't play your trump card of womanhood all the time'** – Apurva feels that women have to work harder than men and it's a given fact. There is no denying it. There is no way a woman can expect fairy tale treatment at all times. She recalls that during her pregnancy, she continued with her work till a week before the D-day. She used to take the local train to work despite her pregnancy, and never expected any special treatment—nor did she get any. Expecting people to alter their behaviour just because you are a woman is not a right expectation, according to Apurva. She feels that women should be very strong and not expect to be treated differently than men. The bottom-line is, 'Because you are a girl, you must resolve to work harder to stay in the game.'
2. **Prioritize your work or career as important as family** – 'There is no either/or when it comes to choosing between family and career. It's AND'—Apurva feels very strongly that girls should really make up their minds on careers and prioritize it like any other priority of their lives. It's better to be determined from the start rather than regretting, that you made sacrifices for your family, later. Many women, who give up on their careers, find it very difficult to bounce back. It's a choice they make but she feels that just because you are a girl, it doesn't mean that only you have to sacrifice your career for everyone else. And once you get that right in your mind, it's easy to go through the process. Reword to The overall percentage of professionally qualified women in the industry is very less anyway". So there is no way an educated working woman should think that she can either have a good career or a

happy family. She should think that she will have a good career AND a happy family. To lead by example—here's how Apurva did it. Get your support system to help you—ask your parents, in-laws etc to help out with kids while you go for work. Request for flexible timings that give you more freedom to do the work at your pace. The cities do offer a system of services that one can use, for example day care centres or part-time nannies. Yes, it will be costly. But to get something, one must be ready to let something go. And by making these choices, one can manage the guilt feeling better. It's like your car. Only when you give the keys of your car to someone else will it get misused. This means that don't give others an opportunity to spoil you or your car. Keep it in your control. Don't let your relatives or neighbours or peers say to you that you are not giving time to your child because of which you begin to feel guilty. You are entitled to your career and your life and you should try your best to make both work. Just don't let the guilt bother you. Only time can prove whether what you did for your family and your own career was good.

When she left Mumbai to Chennai and back to Mumbai because of her husband's job, it was her way to balance both her work and family. She could have easily stayed on in one city and have her husband lead a weekend visit kind of life. But she didn't want to compromise on either her work or her family. So she decided to move to the other city for an equally challenging assignment that gave her best of both worlds. She didn't sacrifice anything.

3. **Spend at least two years in an assignment** – One of the mistakes Apurva thinks she made in her career was to leave Zee prematurely and move to Zoom. She feels that she should have spent more time to make her policies and

bring about the desired changes to make Zee profitable and competitive. But she made a hasty move to Zoom—probably because of the lure of more glamour or pay package. She advises students to spend at least 2-4 years in an assignment depending on the industry.

### Opportunities in Media

The Indian media industry is still very young and evolving every year. Be it the 146 million television households viewing over 6,232 channels, the 82,000 newspapers with a readership of 181.91 million, the approximately 132 million Indian Internet users, or the dozen radio stations heard by millions on either their FM players or cell phones—the reach and exposure provided today by the Indian media, offers unprecedented opportunity to content creators, artistes, audiences, and advertisers alike. The overall industry is pegged at over 1000 billion rupees and has various contributors like TV, print, film, radio, music, OOH, animation VFX, gaming, and digital advertising. If you throw in the telecom factor—smart phones and tablets to this section—the opportunities are spectacular. The various categories of jobs in this sector can be clubbed in the following areas

- Production- this includes artists, scriptwriters, producers, directors, actors
- Operations and management
- Sales and marketing

- Business development
- Technology management
- New initiatives- advertisements over mobile applications
- Online and social media- Facebook, Twitter, LinkedIn, blogging, and much more
- Media buying and strategic planning

(Courtesy KPMG FICCI 2012 report)

# Vivek Sharma PGP '89

## *Chief Marketing Officer Philips India Subcontinent*

VIVEK SHARMA REMEMBERS HIS FIRST real decision on careers when he was in Class 12th. He was a student of Kendriya Vidyalaya in Delhi and like most of us, was asked to take up Mathematics because 'it was imperative for our future and careers', as our parents repeatedly reminded us. He gave the JEE for entrance into IITs but was not selected. He decided to go against his parents' wishes and joined St Stephen's in Delhi. He was elated because he probably thought that instead of writing engineering again, he might be able to finish the course at St Stephen's and later decide on other options. But thanks to pressure from peers and family members, he had to write the engineering exam one more time. This time, he got calls from engineering colleges in Rourkee and Dhanbad (both are now IITs). He had to make a choice between civil engineering in Rourkee and mining in Dhanbad. At that age, it really didn't matter, nor did he have any personal preference. He opted for Dhanbad because the degree offered was BTech; instead of BE in Rourkee.

So in 1983, he landed up in the Indian School of Mines, Dhanbad. In those days, as the country was still in the License Raj, jobs were scarce. But the products of the Indian School of Mines did get picked up by PSUs like Coal India, private companies like TISCO etc. Software industry was also beginning to grow and companies like CMC etc were also quite frequently offering software and systems planning jobs to the mining engineers. Vivek, however, was not too keen about these prospects. Many others wrote exams like GRE, Gate, GMAT, and CAT for further studies. He was confused about his career options. He met some seniors from his college who were now pursuing MBA from IIMs. He spent time with them to understand more about the IIM and the MBA programme. He got really interested when they talked about the marketing subjects, how they learn things like launching a brand, how to create campaigns, advertisements etc—all things that he really enjoyed doing in college fests and in his spare time. For the first time, he saw a streak of light from the far end of the tunnel of his career. He researched more on the IIMs and the CAT and began to prepare for it. By now, he also had offers from CMC in hand to join in their software division in Calcutta. The salary package from CMC was decent and many of the seniors advised him to take it because there was good opportunity to go abroad—especially to the US. After talking to his seniors from college who were in CMC and similar jobs in other software companies, he found out that the job required a lot of technical and engineering work on systems, programming etc.

He thought about which road to take and asked himself 'what motivates me?'—a question he asks himself when he makes his career choices even today. He realized that since he enjoyed doing work which was more creative, applied his faculties of both left and right brain, and helped him learn, the obvious choice was to go for the MBA programme focussing on marketing instead of the software job. So he made the first informed career choice of his life—to write the CAT and try for a place in the IIMs to further marketing.

In 1987, he entered IIM Bangalore. He loved all the marketing related subjects and as time passed, he knew that the kind of job he wanted from the campus had to be in this sector. In those days, finance and consulting were considered top sectors but his heart was set on marketing. He landed three jobs at campus.

One was from Lintas (now LOWE)—an advertising agency and the other two were from UB group (beverage division) and now Mondelez International. He immediately decided to let go of the Lintas offer because he was quite focussed on a marketing job. The Lintas role veered towards advertising which he liked but he wanted to start off on the marketing side first and then possibly explore advertising later. So he turned it down. Now the difficult part came of choosing one between UB and Cadbury. UB was offering a salary significantly higher than Cadbury—one of the highest at the IIMB campus at that time. In those days, there was no LinkedIn or Facebook. There were fewer phones, and emails were not the best way to reach out to someone. So, one had to rely on knowing and meeting people personally. Vivek wanted to consult his seniors again. This was a great blessing for establishing a valuable network for guidance—something that Vivek sees missing in students today. He connected with an alumnus of IIMB working in UB and asked him various questions like—what constitutes a typical day of a marketing job in UB, what does one do, would there be opportunities to launch/relaunch products etc. At the end of this exercise he realized that the job in UB was definitely more glamorous and paid better than Cadbury. But it was also more focussed on managing the distribution and dealers, constrained by regulatory restrictions around liquor sales and marketing, different set of taxation rules in each state which made investment and distribution in each state governed by a different set of considerations. Somehow Vivek wanted to learn the full ambit of marketing and not cut his teeth in a marketing environment which was less than complete. Cadbury on the other hand was in a familiar category with unrestrained and complete FMCG marketing, inspiring leadership at the top and exciting product portfolio but a much smaller pay package. However, the job was what he had hoped to do and read about in the marketing and advertising magazines and classes—classic marketing role of completely managing a brand, campaigns and launching of new products. He once again asked himself, 'What motivates me?'—and the answer was loud and clear—Cadbury.

## The Formative Years

In 1989, he landed himself in the Cadbury office of Mumbai. He was thrilled to work on the flagship Cadbury brands like 'Dairy Milk', 'Eclairs', '5 star', 'Bournvita'—a dream job which he'd wanted to do from his BTech days.

He learned a lot and after about an year or so, a life-changing episode happened. Vivek got a call from a head hunter about a marketing job at one of the world's most reputed MNC banks in India. The pay was a quantum leap from what he was getting at Cadbury and the future career growth seemed to be exponential. He was really tempted and for the first and only time, decided to take up the offer without consulting his seniors in that company or sector. Vivek was enamoured by the fancy title they were offering, the package, and the excitement of the whole experience. He thought that if he got to be a part of the most reputed MNC bank, it would give him more learning and a bigger canvas than what he had. He admits that the pay package also excited him tremendously. So, he moved to that MNC bank.

Within a month, he realized that a marketing job in the banking sector was not the same as a marketing job in Cadbury. While the pay packet was brilliant, the title was fancy, and the glamour quotient was terrific, there was no meaningful work that excited Vivek. He just had to sit there waiting for regulations to be removed from government for the bank to open their new branches, launch new financial products, and their campaigns. He also realized that most decisions were taken in the RBI's office or MNC bank's headquarter outside India. So all he was doing was being a local contact point for the marketing campaigns and a liaison for the agency. He disliked it right from the first week. He sorely regretted leaving Cadbury.

In about two months, he realized that the job was not what he had expected it to be. He was terribly bored. There was absolutely no action in that bank. He sought advice from friends and seniors and expressed his mistake. Thankfully, someone in his friend circle informed back the Cadbury HR head and they called him. Vivek went to the Cadbury office and with a lot of courage and humility acknowledged his hasty decision. The HR head was a very balanced fellow. He asked Vivek, 'Why don't you come back?' and Vivek was stumped. He feared the whiplash waiting for him once he came back—just like how a son runs away from home, realizes his mistake, comes back but is still fearful of entering the house because he knows that the dad will beat him to pulp first and forgive later. The HR head, however, was understanding and told him that they liked his work and that we all make mistakes. As long as Vivek knew what he was doing and was ready to come back with the same zeal and passion, their doors were open. Vivek immediately accepted and joined back at the same position, salary, and project that he was working on in Cadbury. It was like being back after a long leave. The first big lesson of Vivek's working life—do not jump at money or glamorous trappings of a job but for the real job content.

## The Rising Star

Vivek admits that this episode was a very humbling one. His return to Cadbury did have some of his peers and colleagues sniggering at him but he accepted his mistake. He told himself that he deserved this treatment but he also pushed himself to work hard and prove the sceptics wrong. He trudged on, proved himself all over again, and was chosen for the 'Accelerated Development Programme' of the company and asked to move to London. This episode only proves that mistakes are made even by the best. It is how one deals with the mistake—accepting it, keeping one's nose to the ground, and focussing on coming back with results—that matters. Once you show results again, no one really remembers the mistake at all. Vivek says that this episode was never discussed or used as reference point ever in his life at Cadbury after that moment. He moved on and so did everyone else.

He spent around six years at Cadbury. He learnt the ropes of classic marketing jobs and felt that it was time to take his career to the next level. India was growing, especially after the new economic reforms in early nineties. One of the MNCs, Warner Lambert, was setting up its operations in India. They had brands like Chiclets, Clorets, and Halls in their portfolio. He got a call from them to join and he was now ready to take up a new assignment. He spoke to his seniors in the industry and they encouraged his move. So in 1995, he started a new chapter of his career as the head of marketing at Warner Lambert. He successfully launched Clorets in India, doubled the volumes of Halls, and successfully relaunched Chiclets. His skills and expertise got noticed by the top management and he began to move up fast. He was asked to create a three-year business plan for India and present it to the board of the company at New Jersey, USA. This was where he actually applied all the MBA theory and the stint of Cadbury into skills required in a boardroom and transformed himself as a future leader. The plan was approved and Vivek was asked to execute it, which was a big accomplishment for him personally.

By 1999, Warner Lambert was taken over by Pfizer. The acquisition saw a lot of people leaving, new management coming in, and an overall re-prioritization and slowdown in the India plans. His strategic plan that was approved was put on hold and he realized that the new company had bigger issues to deal with globally. India was just a small blip on their map. He decided that it was time to find a new job. Many seniors advised him to wait for couple of years but that was not an option as it didn't motivate him anymore. So he decided to leave without any future plan or job in hand. He knew that he would get many offers but it was time to think upon the next 10 years with a cool mind.

The dot-com boom landed him many attractive opportunities but he just couldn't relate to the idea of working on websites. He was a hard core marketing guy. He couldn't relate to an idea which had no business model (at that time). It was a fluffy make-believe world he didn't quite understand and decided to stay away. He always feels better and prudent to stick to things that he knows and can relate to. Few months passed. He waited patiently. Then one day, he approached Ogilvy (O&M then)—the famous advertising company. His seniors and peers advised him not to take up this advertising job. They had two reservations. One was that he was on the buyer's side of marketing earlier and would hire the services of Ogilvy to do their advertising campaigns; so to move to the services side would be treated as step-down by the market. Second, it would be difficult for him to come back to a sales and marketing job from advertising.

This didn't deter him at all. He thought that if he wanted to be a good marketing person, a stint in advertising was extremely critical. It's a great learning experience to be on the client side of the business, learn about the creative process, and the communications of a campaign. Also it gives a marketing and communication exposure across myriad industries and segments. So he joined Ogilvy in January, 2000. Though he was not immediately sure of his decision, he was patient. In hindsight, this was the best decision that shaped his career. Though he apparently stepped down a little, the rise was even greater once he proved himself. He spent five wonderful years with Ogilvy and finally moved on to being executive director and national head for the entire Hindustan Unilever's account from Ogilvy in India across functions. This stint helped him tremendously in understanding the needs of consumers and broadened his view as he had to now manage various stakeholders and people. He really honed his people management skills in the advertising stint. As a bonus, he understood the depth and intricacies of creative advertising.

In 2005, as the electronics industry of India boomed with the liberalization of policies conducive for import and export, the market exploded with consumer electronics—televisions, white goods like refrigerators, air conditioners, microwaves, washing machines, kitchen appliances etc. He also knew that the next big gap in his career as a marketing guy was sales. He had spent ten years in classic marketing jobs, five years in advertising, and next he wanted to get the sales part covered. He got his chance with Onida (MIRC electronics) where he was offered the opportunity to join as the vice president of sales, marketing, and service. It was a golden chance that allowed him to work on an exciting line of products, new wave of technology and a promising market of the new Indian middle class. Moreover, it was a downright grassroots level sales job. The consumer durable industry is known to be the toughest one for managing sales—the dealers, pricing, margins all changing at a rapid pace. Compared to consumer durables, FMCG seemed like a walk in the park to Vivek. And he took it completely by the horns. He relaunched the famous 'Devil' of Onida television back with a new campaign, and got the after-sales service spruced up. The sales sky rocketed in new categories like air conditioners, microwaves, and within one and half years, Onida's brand recall was one of the highest in India. One blessing of this job was that since he was also heading the after-sales services, he now fully understood the entire gamut of marketing operations which included pricing, distribution, and after-sales services. Onida was probably the only Indian company which was competing with MNCs like Samsung, LG, Whirlpool etc. So it was quite a daunting but rewarding experience that helped Vivek learn some valuable lessons in tight cost management, speed of action, and being adaptive in a highly competitive environment.

Again, most of his peers and seniors from the industry were aghast when he took up the job at Onida. For a marketing guy to move to advertising and then to sales, marketing, and service—that too in the tough durable industry—was unheard of. However, Vivek chose this path based on what he wanted to do. Slowly, he became a role model to all of his peers and seniors, and they started to follow his example.

In 2008, Philips was looking to fill-in their newly created position of chief marketing officer for the Indian subcontinent and Vivek was the candidate unanimously chosen by the global top management. They also mentioned that what made him stick out above everyone else was his diverse background in all disciplines of marketing, sales, advertising, and P&L (Profit & Loss) management.

Vivek joined Philips India in March, 2008 as their first chief marketing officer, responsible for building its overall image in India. He built 'ONE PHILIPS' marketing planning and implementation for the three Philips' businesses viz. consumer lifestyle, lighting, and healthcare. He has been largely instrumental for strengthening the local marketing organization (talent, employee engagement scores), country activation of NPS (Net Promoter Score), marketing intelligence, and building a robust digital presence of the company. Philips enhanced its salience via increased presence in mass media with sponsorship of marquee events like ICC Cricket World Cup 2011 and hiring brand ambassadors like John Abraham and Kareena Kapoor. Since 2008, the Philips brand has entered new segments in home decorative lighting, PC accessories, and personal care. It has enhanced its retail presence and established thought leadership platforms in healthcare. Since 2011, Vivek is also heading the public and professional affairs function of the company that focusses on government relations.

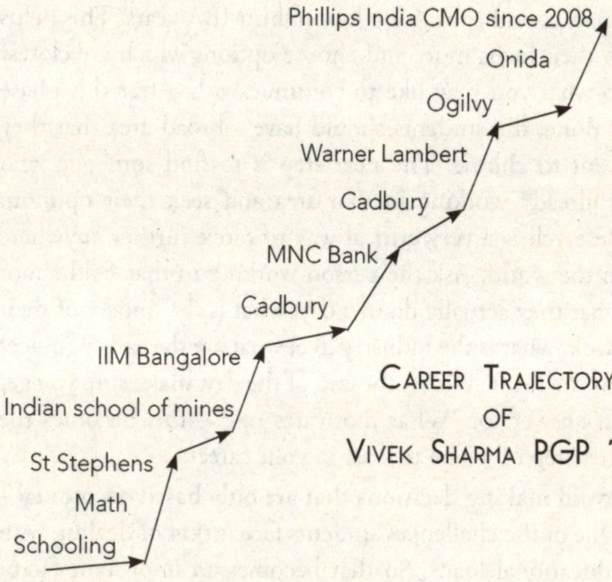


CAREER TRAJECTORY OF VIVEK SHARMA PGP '89

## KEY MESSAGES TO STUDENTS

Vivek gives the following messages for students to think on making career choices.

1. **Ask yourself, 'What motivates me?' Start somewhere –** It's always a chicken and egg problem but you have to start somewhere. The obvious question in the mind of a student which may arise is, 'How does one decide which way to start?' Vivek says that the simplest way is to find a role model out of your family, friends, and social circles—anyone in the world about whom you can say, 'I want to be like him/her.' That's the best starting point to identify a goal. If that is not the case, and the student is not able to decide a role model, then it is best to adopt a negation method which is what Vivek did. He negated biology and arts when he was in his younger years, negated software, finance, and consulting jobs in his MBA years. This helps to then focus more and choose options which are closest to what you may like to continue with. After this phase is done, the students should have a broad area that they want to choose. The next step is to find someone who is already working in that area and seek their opinion. Research is a very critical way to move further anywhere in the world. Ask the person working in that field about what they actually do in a day, what is the impact of their work, what is the industry like, what are the career choices for the future etc. At the end of the day, make sure you get an answer for 'What motivates me?'—this becomes the first step of where to start in your career.
2. **Avoid making decisions that are only based on money –** One of the challenges students face is that of dealing with educational loans. So that becomes an important factor in deciding for jobs. The obvious way is to go for a job which pays more so that the loan can be repaid faster. Vivek disagrees with this approach completely, though. He too had taken a loan for his MBA. He knew that a

bank loan would be stricter as the EMI would kick in after he graduated which could colour his decision. So he took the loan from family friends. The advantage of this is that you can pay the loan at more convenient and flexible conditions that are mutually conducive. So he advises students to explore opportunities where the educational loans can be obtained from friends and family members. This takes away the fear of loan EMIs and can be a blessing in making the right career choices. Vivek also cautions from experience that remuneration and job content are often not in sync. What this means is that the most boring job might be the most lucrative and the most interesting job the least. He suggests to focus on the job content first and then the money. He had a choice to join UB which was paying three times more than Cadbury. But after realizing that the job content was not as exciting or meaningful, he let it go. He feels that it was this thought process that made all the difference in his life.

3. **Choose classic roles of marketing** – Vivek suggests that as much as possible, in the formative years, choose a job that is the classic role of that sector. A classic role in the marketing sector would typically incorporate the famous 4Ps of marketing as defined by Kotler (Kotler, 2003). They would require promotion, pricing, and distribution for a product. For a marketing sector, these jobs are titled quite simply—marketing manager, sales manager, and brand manager etc. These are the jobs which really help you learn the ropes of that sector. They may not sound very fancy as compared to say a friend who decided to go for a job called 'strategic business analyst' or 'assistant vice president of new initiatives'. This is what Vivek learnt from the mistake of joining the MNC bank. Fancy

designations may be attractive, but the core work content is more important. Chances of the assistant vice president polishing power point presentations and spreadsheets for the vice president as his full time job are quite high. So while they sound cool and might give you a great salary, the work might not be exciting at all. The early years of career are quite important in building foundations. It is imperative that one gets to learn different things that help make the foundation stronger. It's like a pyramid. The broader the base, the more robust and bigger the pyramid can be. It gets narrower as you move up. Vivek says that many marketing companies don't even entertain a person for a particular position if the person has not clocked a minimum amount of time in the field with trade partners or direct work with consumers—doing the ground level work is considered de rigueur.

4. **Working in different cultures** – Culture is a set of unspoken rules and way-of-working of a country or an organization. It prepares one to handle global roles better. Working with different organization gives a flavour of the variety of cultures. One learns not only the hard things like cost controls, cash flow, innovation, distribution but also softer aspects like managing owner's expectations, creative cultures (advertising agencies), centrally controlled cultures, numbers driven culture, sales culture, hard task driven ones etc. Each company helped him learn various new aspects of business and life. A creative company like Ogilvy taught him appreciation of working with creative and artistic people, Cadbury UK taught him things like punctuality, eye for detail, wholistic product marketing and being 'proper' in communication. And Onida gave him the experience of working for a family-owned business with a very different style of leadership

as compared to what he had seen in MNCs—speed of action, cost controls, and a challenger mindset.

5. **Whether to stay put or change** – Many students face the dilemma of when to move from the current role that they are doing. Vivek suggests that a good benchmark is to spend at least four years in a relevant job before you think of moving further. He says that if someone has done some work only a year or so, it really doesn't count for much. Focus on building a 'core expertise'. He also suggests that if one has an ambition to be a CXO someday, it is vital that you cover as much ground in the relevant functions of the organizations as possible. It is also important that the movement into other areas is relevant and make a logical build up of the pyramid. For instance he has seen many smart people in marketing suddenly changing their focus on something very niche like brand, sales auditing, or HR. He observed that once they moved into a specialized function, coming back to the 'core function' often became very difficult.
6. **Career planning is not a linear curve** – Like any phase of life; a career does have its ups and downs. Sometimes it can go sideways or become a jagged crooked non-linear curve. Vivek says that students must be very careful with this. Career planning is their own responsibility and they shouldn't expect anyone else to help. Sometimes to go up, one must learn to step down and be willing to treat this as a maze and not a linear curve. Vivek also suggests that many students expect that the organization's HR will chart their career roadmap like a red carpet and all they have to do is walk on it. That's not true. Career planning is very individual driven and companies like those who know where they are going.

## Myths Shattered

1. **Once I make a bad move in my career, I am finished** – Vivek is a good example of how this is not true. He made a mistake—that too a terrible one, in the second year of his career. But he realized it quickly, had the guts to admit it, and managed to bring his career back on track within a few months. It is never too late to admit mistakes. In fact, everyone makes mistakes. The key is to accept them, gracefully find a way to get over them and move on. Never look back. The world is very forgiving. But make sure you don't make the same mistake twice.
2. **Stepping down in a career is suicide** – Many students think that the only way of career ladders is up. Sometimes, when you are asked to do a job that is perceived to be a step-down, you have made a career suicide. Vivek was told the same by his peers when he moved from Warner Lambert to Ogilvy. It was considered a step-down by the market, and it turned out to be the right thing to do in the long run. The same is true when he joined Onida in sales much later in his career. Both the times, he proved everyone wrong. He got the top job in Philips simply because he had taken these tough choices to learn all aspects of marketing, sales, advertising, and P&L management. Sometimes, stepping down or sideways is the best way to jump up to a new growth trajectory. Students should not project their careers as a linear ladder. It is quite a complicated maze and you should look in every direction for the next move. Sometimes, in a maze, one has to take a step-down, or sideways in order to find a new path up to your promised goals.
3. **I must keep everyone informed about my career plans** – Vivek feels that career management is not a social activity.

It is a part of life. Now one doesn't tell everything about one's life to the whole world. There is absolutely no need of declaring plans to everyone. Be discreet about it but also make sure you are not dishonest with those around you. If you want to write CAT for an MBA, there is no reason for you to declare this to your boss. But it also means that you should not lie to your boss when she asks you about your long-term plans for doing an MBA.

### Opportunities in Marketing

A marketing department in every organization is responsible for managing the customers and bringing money to keep the kitchen fire burning. The various kinds of job profiles available in this department are

- Sales and business development
- Product management and marketing
- Marketing communications
- Pre-sales or post-sales
- Customer relationships
- New product initiatives
- Business to Government relations
- Distribution and channel management
- Retail and retail management

# Haragopal M. PGSEM '01

*Senior Vice President Infosys Limited*

Haragopal M. is the senior vice president and global head of Finacle, the banking software division at Infosys Limited. To quote from the Infosys website, Haragopal has been for the last 19 years, part of the core leadership team at Finacle, the banking solution group of Infosys. Finacle is now recognized globally by banks, consultants, and analyst groups as one of the leaders in the core banking space. It has helped banks across the world to power-up their innovation agenda, enabling them to differentiate their products and service, enhance customer experience, and achieve greater operational efficiency. Finacle is now powering 168 banks across 82 countries enabling its customer banks to serve 447 million accounts and 359 million consumers worldwide. 14 percent of the world's banked population is today served by Finacle.

Haragopal's story is an unconventional one that tells the story of hard work, dedication, and determination—three words most people shy away from. He is a proud alumnus of IIM Bangalore's first PGSEM programme batch of 1998-2001, which makes his the perfect chapter for careers in the technology sector.

## The Formative Years

Haragopal's family hails from Vijayawada in Andhra Pradesh. His father worked with the Indian railways, and had three children, of whom Haragopal was the youngest. Owing to the family's modest financial position, Haragopal learnt pretty early in life important lessons that a Spartan lifestyle teaches, for instance, saving for a rainy day. Nonetheless, his parents imbibed in him the values of respect and dignity which are to this day his biggest motivators in life. Haragopal was a bright student, and also excelled in co-curricular activities.

It was during these years in school that Haragopal came across a quote that left a deep impact on him – 'Think. There must be a better way.' This quote became a motivation for him, and he applied it everywhere he went, and still does today. This was also the time when he discovered his love for physics. A particular lesson on levers influenced him greatly and left him thinking about the 'multiplier effect'. *How can I do something that can be multiplied on a factor of more than one so it has a bigger impact?* Talking about this effect, he relates an incident where he put it in practice. In the late seventies, there was a big cyclone that hit the east coast of India. Thousands of people were impacted. Haragopal and his friends decided to go out and help in any way they could. They became information providers to the authorities. Their responsibility was to comb the streets and run back to the police station or the hospital every time they found someone in need of help. This was an age without mobile phones, so the physical act of running back and forth took up a lot of time and could make all the difference between life and death. This gave Haragopal an idea, and initiated him into the hobby of Amateur Radio. Using this technology he was able to provide an alternative communication network for emergency relief operations. What started as a social cause turned into a hobby and went beyond to give a small town boy invaluable global exposure. As a HAM (that's what Amateur Radio hobbyists were known as) he used to DX (make two way radio contact with distant stations) across the continents with many HAMs including the King Hussain of Jordan and many others from different walks of life. He also worked closely with the likes of Rajiv Gandhi (an avid HAM enthusiast himself and a Member of Parliament then) in providing alternative emergency communication network during the 1982 Asian Games.

Like most young people, Haragopal too did not have a career plan when he was in tenth grade. He knew he did not enjoy biology and chemistry but was good at Math, Physics, and languages. He loved reading books, but could only afford low priced Russian ones. Authors like Fyodor Dostoyevsky, Maxim Gorky and Yakov Perelman were some of his favourites. Popular mathematics and science fiction apart, contemporary social issues occupied Haragopal's mind space in his formative years. Literary figures like Chalam (Gudipati Venkatachalam) and Srisri (Srirangam Srinivsarao of *Maha Prasthanam* fame) made a deep impact on him. While most students of his age were cramming text books to score better marks and join prestigious colleges, Haragopal was moonlighting as a sales boy at a book shop without his parent's knowledge. All he wanted was unlimited access to that treasure trove of stories without spending a penny!

Haragopal's quality of walking the road less traveled laid the foundation for his career. Sure enough, it carried through in his corporate career as well. Incidentally, his first brush with the corporate world happened when he spent a couple of months as a summer intern at a private bank just after his tenth grade for a stipend of Rs 8 a day. It was during this time perhaps that Haragopal first started to understand and be impressed by a banker's profession. He saw how a banker could impact society and business by addressing a very important need, namely financial. At the bank, Haragopal was given a seemingly simple but time consuming task of counting coins that were deposited by a church in four large sacks. No young man would admittedly like to spend his days stacking coins, and Haragopal saw this as an opportunity to implement his philosophy of 'Think. There must be a better way.' He requested his supervisor for permission to use the weighing scales lying in the bank, which were otherwise used only for an hour or two a day to determine postage for letters and parcels. He sampled a few heaps first to get the measure right and then validate. He had hit upon the perfect solution! From there on, he could have offered to count even a hundred sacks and called it child's play. He completed the four sacks way ahead of time. And such was his conviction in his *smarter way* that he even offered to make good for any shortfall from his stipend. Impressed by his thinking, diligence and academic performance (he ranked among the top three at school in tenth grade) the bank manager offered him a job as a junior clerk. While his father encouraged him to take up the job because of his family's modest financial status, some timely advise by a family friend led to Haragopal turning it down and going on to college to study Physics, Math, and Chemistry. However, this decision of choosing a college education over a *safe* job at a bank weighed on Haragopal's thoughts and taught him to be frugal with his father's money for the rest of his student years.

He did well enough in college and got a call from an engineering institution for admission. However, destiny had other plans for him. As he boarded the train, his bag with all his education certificates went missing. The college wanted originals and he was unable to produce them. While it seemed like a blow then, Haragopal was undeterred. Due to the delay in engineering admissions that year, as a safe bet, he had already enrolled in the prestigious Loyola College that year to pursue his first love, Physics. In spite of his father's insistence that he apply for engineering the following year, Haragopal decided to prove that he was better off with a BSc. During those three years at Loyola he was exposed to something that would become a key influence in his life: the armed forces. He joined the Naval wing of NCC (National Cadet Corps) as a student cadet. He loved the planning and discipline of making things happen and also loved the crisp white uniform and shining leather boots. Here, he also discovered the engineer inside him. He developed a keen interest in ship modeling and created many working models to represent his state in the national NCC meets at Delhi. He went on to become the Cadet Captain of the college and was among the 50 cadets chosen nationwide to train on the warships during the summer break.

After graduating in Physics, Haragopal was again at cross roads. He had offers that ranged from MTech in geophysics to MBA at prestigious B schools. The lure of making a high impact in society and the country led him to enroll for post-graduation in Physics at Delhi University, so that he could explore the civil services option. Meanwhile, his earlier resolve to go light on his father's wallet continued to play strongly on his mind, and he took up a morning job at a prestigious school to teach Math and Physics. Haragopal no doubt had high aspirations and ideals and a mind of his own, but he had his logic straight, when you are from a modest financial background, and have chosen an unconventional career path, you need a plan B to stay afloat. The teaching job was supposed to be a way to make money, but it turned out to be much more than that. Along with his students he learnt a lot of interesting things that he missed out on as a small town boy during his school days.

Owing to this, and to the 'hedge advice' by his roommate and alter ego, Haragopal continued to try out different career options even though he aspired to join the civil services. This yet again presented him with a problem of plenty; he had to choose from four offers. Three of them to be a probationary officer at the State Bank group as well as other state owned banks and one as an assistant commandant in the coast guard. After a quick reality check of the offers and analyzing which job best aligned with his ideals and career philosophy, Haragopal chose to join a public sector bank as a probationary officer and started his *Bharat Darshan* period of two years at a rural branch near Bangalore. He loved the fact that he was making an impact in the grass root banking work and was thrilled to learn the various aspects of banking. It is common knowledge that when you join as a direct recruit officer, you are getting ahead of thousands of existing employees who are aspiring for the same role. This was evident from the start when Haragopal was playfully challenged by his colleagues on his very first day as a trainee officer. He responded well by multi-tasking as a teller in the morning, a loan officer in the evening and tending to back office duties as night, thus earning the respect of his new colleagues on day one, and he was accepted into the league. Through all of this, his mind continued to be on overdrive to find ways to make things simple, minimizing the drudgery so his colleagues could spend more face-time with customers rather than papers and computers.

While at the bank, Haragopal once again brought into play his knack for using technology and fueling automation in order to simplify internal operations and maximize customer face-time. One day the bank manager asked him to balance ledgers. In a banking system, this is one of the most labourious tasks done every quarter. In the pre-automation era, it was grueling manual work but extremely important in a bank. Most bankers those days took pride in their ability to add double or even triple digits and balance the ledgers in quick time. Haragopal says that it seemed like criminal waste of time, akin to trying to slay a dragon with a pin rather than a sword. He thought if the job could be done faster; the extra time could be used to identify inconsistencies if any. In those days, every bank branch had an adding machine—which was kind of a basic calculator with a printing roll to print the numbers. Instead of writing the numbers down by hand in the balancing register, he keyed in those account balances into the adding machine and pasted the thin strip of print with balances and totals in the register, tallied the numbers and signed off. This saved time and ruled out the possibility of errors. The next morning, he told his supervisor that he had finished all the ledgers. The supervisor was appalled and pulled him up for his 'laziness'. But when Haragopal explained the benefit of technology and pointed out the time saved for the bank, she was very impressed. Haragopal then became the 'go-to' guy in the branch to simplify things. It was perhaps matter of serendipity that Haragopal, along with a handful of probationary offices who topped the batch were chosen for the technology division. The bank wanted to infuse young blood into the system to develop branch automation software products.

Again, Haragopal was doing what he loved. He was seduced by the idea of making systems which could simplify banking in thousands of branches and dived deep into hardcore programming and designing systems. Over a period of time he became an expert in databases like Oracle and started designing systems for the international operations. Soon enough, he did something unusual. Even while riding the technology wave and making an impact on several bank branches by transforming their business, he signed up for evening classes in law at the Delhi University. Those days, the 'eveningers' had the rare opportunity of learning from both top notch academics and high profile practitioners. In hindsight, he feels, this was one of the best decisions he ever took. His vision was clear, he says that as one advances to leadership and business roles, one needs to know the law of the land well to be an ethical and compliant business leader.

By the early nineties Haragopal had everything going well for him – a well settled family with two tiny tots, a comfortable home, respect and adulation for his work, and his much vaunted multiplier effect by transforming many branches through the adoption of branch automation. All these successes however did not satiate him, but fuelled him further to reach the next stage—and now the question was how could he take the benefits of his work beyond a single bank, to many more. He landed offers from three good technology companies– one, to run a large technology project for a client in the US, second to start a database technologies related practice in Mumbai and the third and most exciting, to be part of a product development team in Bangalore. He picked the third, and the company was Infosys.

## The Rising Star

In 1993, if you asked a well-settled bank officer to join a software company, in all likelihood you'd get a stare if not outright ridicule. It is said that most fathers gladly gave their daughters in marriage to guys with bank jobs. Haragopal wanted to design world-class software products to make life simpler and better for millions; so, he chose Infosys. Haragopal believes that choosing the right company is like choosing the right life partner; once you've made the choice, you stick by it through thick and thin. At Infosys, Haragopal was the only non-engineer, but his rich experience in banking software came in handy for the job. The company was working on a banking product, and Haragopal was the perfect addition to the family. He started his innings at Infosys by jumping into the deeper side of the pool. His first responsibility was to port the banking solution that was being piloted in one bank in India to three different operating system platforms to produce the first GA version (a version of software product for General Availability for distribution to multiple clients) of the product Bancs2000. And of course, all of it was to be accomplished in the first 100 days of his starting at the job. Instead of being daunted by the task, Haragopal got an adrenalin rush from the challenge.

He moved his family out the bank quarters, took up a simple residence, didn't even bother to buy furniture, and faced the challenge head on. His team and he toiled hard, only returning home in the mornings to shave and shower. Finally the product was ready for distribution on time as promised.

When his father asked Haragopal how his new workplace, Infosys, was, his answer was simple, 'The best is ordinary here.' The Indian IT story was just beginning to shape up and Haragopal was at the helm of this ship. Between 1993 and 1998, he laid the foundation for Finacle as a product—he took on multiple roles including domain chief, program manager and the like in product development and engineering, and defined frameworks, processes, and built core functionalities like multi-currency and universal banking to name a few.

In 1998, he was asked by his mentor, a member of the board to make a lateral shift to head the customer engagements and delivery side of the banking business unit. This was something Haragopal had never done before. This was a crucial stage for the business, and it needed someone to lay the foundation for a professional services organization that could drive large scale core banking transformation programs. At heart, he was a technologist, comfortable with codes and engineers. With customer engagements, though, he was asked to take a leap of faith and move to an area he had no clue about—business. He took on the challenge knowing fully well that he had a steep learning curve ahead. His formula for excellence was simple: Learning Opportunity (LO) is the gap between one's current capability to do things (CC) and what is actually required to reach one's goal (RC). For those who love math, here is the simple mathematical representation that Haragopal follows

$$RC - CC = LO$$

He signed up for the PGSEM program at IIMB to address the LO. He was on the road three days a week, did assignments at airports or on flights, and sometimes arrived at the classroom straight from the airport and went home later to immerse his head in his new learning. Between 1998 and 2007, he grew Finacle's foot print to many countries and went on to become its global head. By 2012, Finacle's revenue multiplied by three times. Today, Finacle touches approximately 14 percent of the world's banked population.

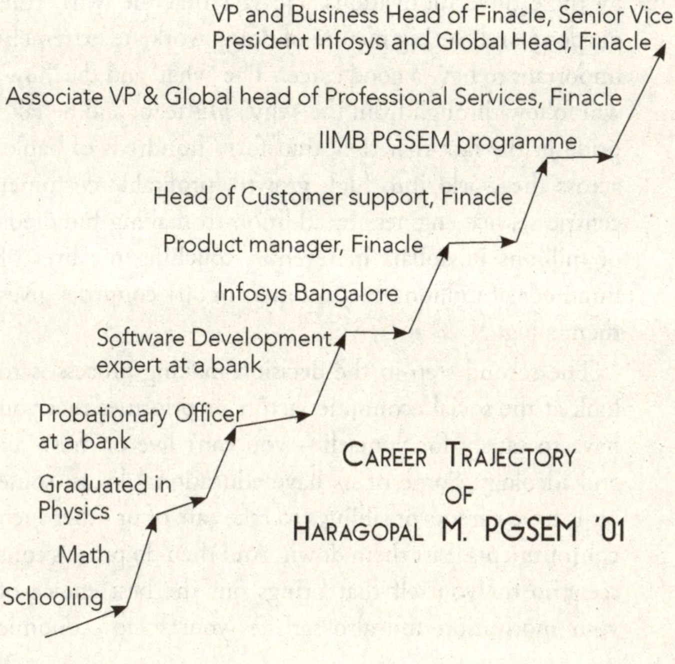


CAREER TRAJECTORY OF HARAGOPAL M. PGSEM '01

## Key Messages to Students

1. **Find out what motivates you** – Haragopal suggests a two-step method to finding an answer to the question 'what motivates me'. The first stage is to list down factors. For Haragopal some of his motivations were:

    a. To be in a team or environment where the best is ordinary
    b. To learn incrementally but improve exponentially
    c. To have a multiplier effect or breakthrough impact

    Right from childhood, in all his decisions, there was a method to the madness: all of his choices were driven by these three motivations. He says that the 'why' (the purpose) and the big picture of doing work are extremely important to have a good career. The 'what' and the 'how' will follow through from the 'why'. His team and he take pride in the fact that they transform hundreds of banks across the world into high growth, profitable customer centric service engines. In addition to making hundreds of millions in dollars in revenue, touching the lives of hundreds of millions of consumers in 80+ countries gives them a high.

    The second step in the decision making process is to look at the social economic factors or priorities that you have to satisfy for yourself – you can't live on fresh air and ideology. Some of us have educational loans; some of us have parents or siblings to take care of or other such commitments. List them down. And then do pros vs cons scenario for yourself that brings out the best choice of your motivation and also satisfies your socio economic obligations—having a plan B to meet the obligations actually gives you the freedom to take more risks.

2. **Always back yourself and take calculated risks** – According to Haragopal the biggest difference between you and the millions of others around you with similar degrees and titles is your ability to take risks. If he had not taken the risk of letting go of a teaching job in Delhi in 1986, or the powerful coast guard job, and then opting out of the secure PSU banking job for a less known company in the private sector—he wouldn't have been where he is today. Your career choices are ultimately your decisions since you have a 360 degree view of yourself. While you can take inputs from anyone – don't lean on or blame anyone else for your career choices. He says, 'play to your wrong hand till 40. After 40, play to your strong hand.' This means, experiment with all the things you want to try out before you turn 40. After that, choose something that you are really good at, which is your strength.
3. **Degrees are not important. Learning and skills are** – Your career is not a hundred meter sprint, it's not even a marathon but a pentathlon—you need different skills at different stages of your career and you need to spot them early and leverage the learning opportunities. Haragopal's life is the perfect example of learning skills along the way and leveraging them for the best opportunities. From Amateur Radio Ham and part time LLB, to part time software courses and the MBA, his focus was on learning new skills that he could apply to *make an impact.* While most people take up degrees just to land lucrative jobs, what is important is the skill to get the work done. A degree is merely a filter and cannot be the factor for a job opportunity.

## Myths Shattered

1. **Engineering is the only and fastest way to landing a job** – Haragopal started working at a very young age. He promised his dad after he lost his engineering seat that he could prove that he would earn faster and better than all his engineering friends. And he proved himself right. The mathematics of degrees is not the best way to decide careers. Many students that we found in our research chose engineering just because it was a four year path to a job while an MBBS took five, followed by specialization and super specialization that adds up to at least 9-11 years before you start to earn. What matters is your motivation for the job; not how early you bag it. What's the point of being a bad engineer when you could be a good doctor? So if your motivation is to bag a job, there are many options other than engineering. The argument of choosing a degree because it is a fastest way of landing a job is flawed. Haragopal proves that once the motivation is clear, the degrees don't really hinder your progress.
2. **Part time courses don't help** – Again, this is proven wrong by Haragopal. His stellar performance in his career is not because of his degrees. It was because of his sheer determination, knowledge, risk taking, and the skills that he learnt from his educational background. He did a part time LLB and a part time MBA, but made sure he took these courses to learn and help him work better. It takes a lot of effort to put together a sales proposal of $100 million and that's where the PGSEM course provided a great platform for him to learn the ropes of business, sales, marketing, and strategy and apply all of them at Finacle. The LLB helped him understand all the laws of international markets that Finacle operated in. The results are evident today.

3. **Modest economic background means limited opportunities –** Coming from a pre-Internet era, where access to information was very limited in the hinterland, even a small town boy like Haragopal gained good exposure with sheer determination. He studied in a vernacular medium until his $12^{th}$ grade but all he needed was access to a small transistor radio to listen to the BBC radio late in the evenings to improve his language skills. Even with his modest economic means, he could develop some exquisite hobbies like ship modeling and amateur radio which were accessible only to the urban rich those days.

---

**CAREERS IN IT/TECHNOLOGY**

There are myriad jobs in the IT sector

**TECHNICAL JOBS**

- Application Management Services- Application development, application maintenance, application support, application reengineering
- Managed Services- Email management, data management, business analytics
- Infrastructure Management- Server management, data management, security management, desktop management, asset management and system services
- Business Process Outsourcing- Call center services, transaction processing services, verification and validation services
- Technical Communication- Technical writer, API writer, instructional designer, SEO/ content writer, technical editor, corporate communicator and usability expert

---

MANAGEMENT/BUSINESS JOBS

Client engagement- sales, pre-sales, post sales, business development

People management- managing teams, recruiting, training, leadership and development

New product development and consultancies

Others- Project management, program management, knowledge management, sales Enablement, Corporate functions, operations management

Corporate communication, Media and PR management, world conferences

IP creation and promotion- patents, collaborations

Strategic relation management with partner companies

## Rajiv Maliwal PGP '85

*Founder and Managing Partner Sabre Partners*

Rajiv Maliwal, distinguished alumnus of the PGP '85 batch of IIMB, is the founder and managing partner of Sabre Partners, an investment group which has funded and led many startups and late stage companies in India in the areas of financial services, healthcare, and infrastructure. Rajiv has led investments of over US$ 400 million and harvested over US$ 2 billion over the past eleven years, across several companies.

Prior to founding Sabre Partners in 2002, Rajiv was at Standard Chartered PLC as global head of private equity. He raised an over US$ 300 million fund, built a global team, and invested internationally with a focus on financial services and technology. Between 1993 and 1998, he was an executive director at Goldman Sachs, Hong Kong and JP Morgan, Singapore and was responsible for setting up and growing the investment banking and securities businesses for them in India. He established a joint venture for both these firms in India with domestic partners, led many M&As, equity and debt underwritings for Indian corporate, and created several private equity investments. Prior to 1993, Rajiv was with Citibank, where he was responsible for corporate and investment banking in western India.

### The Formative Years

Rajiv had a childhood dream to join the Indian Army. Though he had no member in his family who was in the defense sector, he was enamoured by them. He was born in a time when the country saw two wars—in 1969 with China and 1971 with Pakistan. His icon was Field Marshall Maneckshaw. His schooling was in Kendriya Vidyala in Mumbai where he was surrounded by children from families of the armed forces and navy sector. In 1976, he applied to the NDA and was rejected in the medical test because of poor eyesight. His childhood dream shattered and he got his first taste of failure. He took some time to get over this episode and consoled himself that he was born with those eyes and it was beyond his control. So he recalibrated his career track and focussed on his studies. He liked Biology a lot. But in those days, he didn't have much information on the world of medicine as compared to engineering. So he chose Math to pursue engineering over medicine as a career option.

So in 1978, Rajiv joined BITS Pilani for the engineering programme. In those days, it was a five-year programme. The best feature of the course in BITS Pilani is that they didn't give a choice to a student coming from Class 11th or 12th to choose a branch at that time. The first two years are generic for everyone entering that college. This gives a wonderful platform for students to decide what best suits them based on two years of academic performance, interests, and meeting seniors from different branches. The first two years are so flexible that students can choose any subjects they like from liberal arts, science, and engineering disciplines. This 'menu system' was exactly what Rajiv needed to learn various things beyond engineering and also expand his thinking. He explored the world of computers, mechanical, electrical, electronics and enjoyed them all. This was the time computers were just picking up and was considered a super cool branch to be in. But he somehow was more fascinated by pumps, motors, things that he could actually look at and touch in a lab. So he decided to choose Mechanical Engineering in his 3rd year.

He really enjoyed the engineering subjects and was able to understand how complex manufacturing systems come together to produce cars, tractors, pumps—things we see every day around us. He also learnt a little about computer programming. By now, a new world opened up to Rajiv. The world of business, commerce and international trends which he saw through the *Economic Times* that would come in the college. This was a world he had never seen and he loved reading about what companies were doing to grow businesses, how government policies were shaping industries and so on. He began to understand the financial world, stock markets, economic policies, international trade scenarios, industrialists, exchange rates, gold prices and began to hold focussed group discussions on these topics for juniors. He took avid interest in the manufacturing sector and the going ons in companies like Tata, Eicher etc. Pilani was totally cut-off from civilization. There were no televisions in those days. The nearest cities were either Delhi or Jaipur and they were at least six hours away by bus. So *Economic Times* was the channel that brought in the whole world to Rajiv in Pilani.

When the time came for campus placements, he got a job in TCS which was still a very new company. His decision to apply for TCS stemmed from some seniors mentioning potential travel opportunities—mostly to the US. Since he had read so much about American multinational companies, he was very keen to see and explore the US further. Moreover, his heart was now set on a career in the world of business. The jobs in the mechanical sector would not have taken him closer to that world—at least in the short-term. He had offers from Escorts and Eicher—two of the top companies in India that time for the mechanical engineering jobs. He also thought about GMAT or CAT for an MBA but felt that it would be better to work for a few years first.

So from the various roads he had in front of him in the final year of his engineering, he decided to join TCS Mumbai in 1982. Within the first few months, he realized that he didn't like what he was doing. He was put in a long training programme and even made to write tests to clear for getting certified in certain programming skills. He did quite badly on the test and based on the scores, he was then put in a project which he thought was quite boring. It took him few days to realize that this is not what he wanted to do in life. The world of finance, business that he loved was so far away and he knew he had to find a road heading in that direction. The options in front of him were few—either an MBA programme abroad or in India. In those days, IIMs were not as popular as they are today. They were also very focussed on the public sector industries. But his mind was made up. The only way for him to come closer to his dream of finance and business was MBA. So he wrote the CAT and joined IIM Bangalore in 1983.

The class of PGP '83-85 had a wide variety of people from different ages, backgrounds, and interests. He was very happy to have had made this choice. He was a good all-round student. He excelled in sports and participated in all cultural events amongst IIMs as well. He particularly enjoyed the finance subjects and it fuelled his desire to work closer to the financial world. His favourite subject was Accountancy in the first year by Prof Prasanna Chandra. He did very well at it and in time was able to understand the *Economic Times* much better as he could understand the balance sheets of the company, and terms used like PE/Debt ratio, EBITDA etc. This further motivated him to explore options in finance. Thanks to the environment of IIM Bangalore, he got some clarity on what kind of a job he wanted for his summer internship and final placement. He wanted to join a bank. This is the year 1984 we are talking about—the Stone Age for the MBA world in India. Most of the jobs available in the country were in the public sector. There was no term called 'consulting' or 'private equity' or 'investment banking' in those days. The marketing and FMCG sector was mushrooming and Rajiv signed up for a short project with one of the companies. Though he enjoyed the project he did for them, and was good at social interaction, meeting people, and making sales pitches, he felt that a sales or marketing job was not his cup of tea. His heart was fixed on the world of finance and banking. He aspired for a summer internship at Citibank.

To explain how Rajiv felt for Citibank, recall the famous story of Arjuna, one of the Pandava brothers, and the challenge from his Guru to shoot the eye of the wooden bird with his arrow. All the disciples queued up. Guru Dronacharya asked them one by one as they got ready to shoot, 'What do you see?' Yudhishtra said, 'I see the jungle, sky, and the trees.' Bhima said, 'I see the tree and its leaves.' When Arjuna's turn came, he replied, 'I see the eye of the bird. Nothing else.' That's exactly how Rajiv saw Citibank.

Citibank was a very tough company to get in to. They would comb all the top campuses and barely take 6 or 8 in all for their summer internship programme. Traditionally, most of these interns also made it to the final placement. It was considered a tough one to crack. Rajiv had set his goal though and worked hard. He researched the kind of questions that were typically asked, brushed up his financial concepts, macroeconomic environment of business, government policies, and the latest trends of corporate banking that would help in the growth of banking services in India. He even learnt how to wear a tie properly. He left no stone unturned to be prepared for the interview. During the interview, Rajiv did quite well; he was absolutely confident and calm. Fortune favours those who are prepared. Rajiv was the only one from IIMB who got the coveted internship in Citibank by his laser focus and his preparedness.

The two months of summer internship in 1984 were wonderful. Rajiv felt elated to be in the coveted club. Being the only one from IIMB in that programme, he got his first taste of success through sheer focus and hard work. He was made to do a project using his computer skills that he had acquired in BITS and TCS. The task was to automate the letter of credits to a database and finally making a computer generated printed copy. Though this had nothing to do with financial aspects of a bank, Rajiv knew that this was just a testing ground for him to demonstrate his abilities. He enjoyed working with his peers and seniors. A big learning in this phase was that in campus, the Citibankers were treated like god; but up close they seemed as humans as anybody else. This also improved his self-confidence and he made good friends with many of them. The summer project that he was supposed to do, though, did not go very well. He got an average rating at the end of the internship.

Rajiv now looks back at those days and thinks that the success of making into Citibank summer placement programme went to his head. He was the coolest dude on campus and his friends also heralded the achievement. He was confident that he would get the final placement offer from Citibank as well. He loosened up a little. He slacked on his $2^{nd}$ year at IIMB thinking that he had a secure job at Citibank because historically, most of the summer placement candidates got the offer to join after the MBA is over. He assumed that he too would make it. His dreams crashed when Citibank came for final placements and announced the list of selected candidates. His name was on the wait list. This came as a double whammy. Before he could recover from this jolt, he suddenly realized that he had not applied to any other company for a final job. This was the end of the MBA programme and not many companies were lined up. Imagine a rising star and then imagine its spectacular crash. That's how Rajiv felt at that time. From being the coolest dude at campus who cracked the most coveted summer placement offer, to being a student who didn't have any confirmed job in his hands at the end of the programme.

This was a massive humbling experience for Rajiv that built his foundation of leadership for future. Just a few days before, he was on top of the world. And then it seemed a tornado just whizzed past, and left nothing but shattered dreams in its wake. He learnt the invaluable lesson of staying focussed and not to slacken our efforts. His win on summer placements caused him to slacken his pace and lose focus on the final placements. The results were right in front of him. He took some days to play the entire episode all over again in his mind, spent a lot of time introspecting. His friends became his support system. Thankfully, his future wife Srividya, who was in the first year of the MBA programme as well, was strong as a pillar to him those days. He came out of this episode and was ready to take on the challenge once again. He applied to a few companies through personal contacts and got through a reputed company of the Tata Group—Eureka Forbes.

However, he did not lose sight of Citibank. He stayed in touch with his seniors who gave him feedback on why he was not selected. He took that very positively and dedicated his attention to the job at Eureka Forbes. He also kept his managers there informed about his desire to work for the financial world. His boss encouraged him to keep trying with Citibank in case a suitable opportunity opens up. The job at EF was not exactly what he loved doing. EF as a company was in direct selling of products like water purifiers, vacuum cleaners etc. When Rajiv was in BITS, he had done a summer project with DCM where his job was to go door-to-door, selling calculators of DCM. In two months, after knocking about few thousand doors in the apartments of Mumbai, he managed to sell one piece. That learning came in handy at EF. He was involved in making plans and focussed group surveys to come up with better ideas to increase sales.

In just six months, Citibank asked Rajiv to join the company. Citibank was growing its commercial banking in a big way and the timing was just right. Rajiv said a big 'yes' and found himself back in his dream company keeping in mind the first big lesson of his life—never lose focus and accept defeat. If the doors are closed, break a wall to get through.

Life at Citibank was not at all rosy for Rajiv. First of all, he was six months behind his peers from other MBA schools and hence was not part of their clique. They all had been sent to Manila for a long induction programme. They all bonded quite well and Rajiv was an outcast to this group. He felt lonely. His first job at Citibank was to sit in the back office and issue duplicate demand drafts for the corporate clients. He asked himself, 'What am I doing here?' Any MBA from a top school would probably ask the same question too. But Rajiv told himself that this is the world's number one bank. There must be a reason for it to be such a good company. He mentally programmed himself to be patient, do the work at hand to the best of his ability, and stick on for a while. His patience started bearing fruit and from the back end job, he moved to the front desk. Then slowly he started to lead a team of people doing the banking operations. He later realized that this exposure to running the operations gave him a strong foundation of the banking world. This rich knowledge would prove valuable later on in his career.

One day, his boss called him to discuss an opportunity in the Delhi office. Citibank had just launched its new cash management product and needed someone to manage this for the Delhi market. In those days, the financial city of India was Mumbai. Delhi was considered the boondocks and no one in Citibank would want to go there for the fear of getting stuck. But Rajiv thought of this as an opportunity. Citibank Mumbai was no doubt the safe shining ivory tower—anyone would give an arm or leg to be there. Rajiv felt that it was better to be the king of the boondocks than a nobody in the ivory tower. So he moved lock, stock and barrel to India's capital and began building Citibank's portfolio from scratch. He had a wonderful boss who supported all his innovative plans. This two-year effort of converting the Delhi office into a productive office, bringing in more clients, and increasing revenue for Citibank got him the much needed recognition and he was called back to the Mumbai office in 1990.

His reward was to be the account manager of the most prestigious corporate house of India—Tata Group. When he first visited the famous Bombay House, the headquarters of Tata Group, he felt very intimidated. He felt like a small boy among grownups. He also realized that if he had to do a good job, he had to be thorough with the entire technical part of banking that Tata Group would want him to do for them. He knew how to handle customers and manage relationships; but he did not know the whole chain of corporate lending process that he was supposed to handle with Tata. So he became a student once again, spent hours pouring over literature of this subject, policies of Citibank, experiences of his seniors, and armed himself with knowledge—again to be better prepared to handle his dream customer's requirements.

He grew from the position of account manager to head of customer relationships of west India—that accounted for roughly 40 percent of Citibank India's revenues from corporate banking. This was the beginning of Rajiv's career in the stadium of deals, mergers, acquisitions, funding, and investments—the playground for international business. For the first time in his life, Rajiv was rewarded handsomely for his efforts. India was just beginning to open up to foreign investment, the entire world was looking this way and Rajiv was sitting pretty on the largest opportunity on offer. He noticed a new trend in the banking sector. Corporate banking was definitely hot, but a new slew of incumbents called investment banks started to show in Bombay House—the headquarters of Tata, and Rajiv's marquee account at Citibank. He would see them in swanky suits walking into the CFO's office while he waited outside. He began to research on this new trend and found that there were global names like Goldman Sachs, Solomon Brothers, Credit Suisse, Merrill Lynch etc in this space. They would offer strategic guidance to companies along with money and help scale the business further. These were the mega billion dollar deal makers of the world.

The more he researched about this space, the more he longed to be a part of the action. He found that these organizations hired the best from around the world. Their teams comprised of alumni from Harvard, Stanford, Wharton etc. Each deal would be so impactful that it could alter the course of business history. These folks were professionals who were also clued in the world macro-economic situation, wrote books that influenced policies, and were thought leaders in their field. They were slick salesmen and very powerful bankers as well—each managing a portfolio that was more than the GDP of many third-world countries.

He met a few of them through personal connections to understand what they did and soon enough was spotted by many head hunters in this area. Though he had no prior exposure in investment banking, his exposure to corporate banking and understanding of Indian customers made him just the right candidate for their India strategy. In a span of few months, he got interview calls from the world's best investment banks. He was invited to meetings in Hong Kong in a private jet and the meetings lasted all day to dinner and cocktails. He first got an offer from GE Capital, which was immediately followed by Credit Suisse, and UBS.

One day, he was on a flight back to Mumbai after meeting Credit Suisse, a tall gentleman walked up to his seat in the plane and introduced himself as one of the king makers in the banking world. He requested Rajiv to attend one more interview back in Hong Kong. The company that was interested was the one Rajiv was looking for—Goldman Sachs. So Rajiv landed in Mumbai and was back on a flight to Hong Kong the next day. This was another big milestone in Rajiv's life. Just like how he was focussed and prepared for Citibank when he was in IIMB, he was prepared and ready for this call from Goldman Sachs. They loved him and made him an offer that made every other offer look inadequate in every aspect. Rajiv felt that he made the second mistake of his life that day—by accepting the offer without really knowing how to do the work of an I Banker. It was like being asked to drive a Cessna without any prior training and assuming that if you know how to drive a car, you could handle a Cessna aircraft as well.

The job offer from Goldman Sachs was just too good to be true. To be selected was another feather in his hat. He probably was the first person from India to have made it to that league. He shifted base from Mumbai to Hong Kong in 1993 as the executive director of Goldman Sachs. Till then, he knew how to do corporate banking. But this work in I Bank was a completely different ball game. Rajiv was not prepared for it at all. At that level, one can't even walk up to the boss and ask them for training for the job. So, he struggled to make his presence felt. The world of mergers, acquisitions, and investments is very different from that of corporate banking. Rajiv pulled up his socks and dived into student mode again. He got his hands dirty in the entire process, sat down and poured over the entire methodology, spent time with the experts and began to climb the ladder slowly. He worked closely with many customers in India, gave them strategic and financial advice on the impact of privatization in their work. He also consulted many PSUs on the globalization phenomenon that India was about to enter into. He learnt another important lesson in this experience—never to rest on one's laurels. Another important thing that Goldman Sachs taught him was the importance of peer review. It's not only results that matter, relationships matter too. Your peers, superiors, and subordinates all have a say in your evaluation. Your success is also defined by what *you* did and what *others* think you did.

In 1997, his name was counted in the big league of investment bankers in the Asian region. He joined JP Morgan that same year to head their entire South East Asia office. This time he was better prepared to enter JPM as compared to GS. He did lot of research on what he is supposed to do and made his presence felt by setting up a joint venture with ICICI to start the JPM broking securities operations for India. By 1999, Rajiv's career trajectory had taken a wonderful shape. He had done thorough ground work in corporate banking followed by investment banking. However, he was more of a transaction specialist, a deal-maker of repute. The time had come for him to take on a larger role and gun to be a CEO of a large financial organization. He didn't have to wait too long, either.

Grindlays India was one the largest private banks in India in the late nineties. It had 56 branches, 3000 people throughout India in 12 cities. Their current CEO was retiring; and Rajiv was offered to step into his shoes. In comparison, Citibank was a much smaller operation—just 6 branches in 4 cities. This was a role of a lifetime. All departments reported to him and he enjoyed the stint in dealing with people, building teams, drafting a vision for the next decade, working with RBI and the government bodies, and had a wonderful time learning a new phase of business leadership. ANZ, the controlling company for Grindlays Bank, sold off its stake to Standard Charted bank. Rajiv spearheaded the entire merger that took about two years. At the end of this, he was made the global head of private equity and e-commerce division of this combined entity. Though he was not too happy with this and was expecting to be made the CEO, he took this new assignment as a challenge as the space of private equity was just beginning to mushroom—owing to the dot-com boom and bust.

In 2000, the world changed dramatically. The internet revolution had kick started from the Silicon Valley. There were a new breed of young and bright technology entrepreneurs , and venture capitalists who were investing in them. The VCs were ex-investment bankers too. Many of them had started boutique private equity funds as well. So there was a lot of action in this sphere and Rajiv wanted to explore his hand in that. So he was given a kitty of $300 million by Standard Chartered to invest in the e-commerce space. Though he enjoyed meeting young bright minds, somehow he couldn't quite relate to the mechanics of a website, HTML, APIs, etc and the whole value chain of technology. Also by this time, there were changes in the CEO levels of Standard Charted globally and he felt it was time for him to move on.

In 2003, Rajiv started his own private equity firm called Sabre Partners. Over the past decade Sabre has worked to identify, invest in, and enhance the value of great management teams and businesses, large and small. It originated and led the biggest banking roll ups in India and delivered a return which is rated as the best ever in Asia for this industry. Sabre has led a startup in Asset Management in India as a joint venture with Temasek, Singapore. It has also built a fund management business, which was successfully raised and now manages two private equity funds in the infrastructure and healthcare sectors. The healthcare fund has a dedicated capital pool of $50 million, which Sabre is utilizing to back teams who are building healthcare services businesses in India. Sabre also manages an absolute return India-focussed hedge fund.

## Key Messages to Students

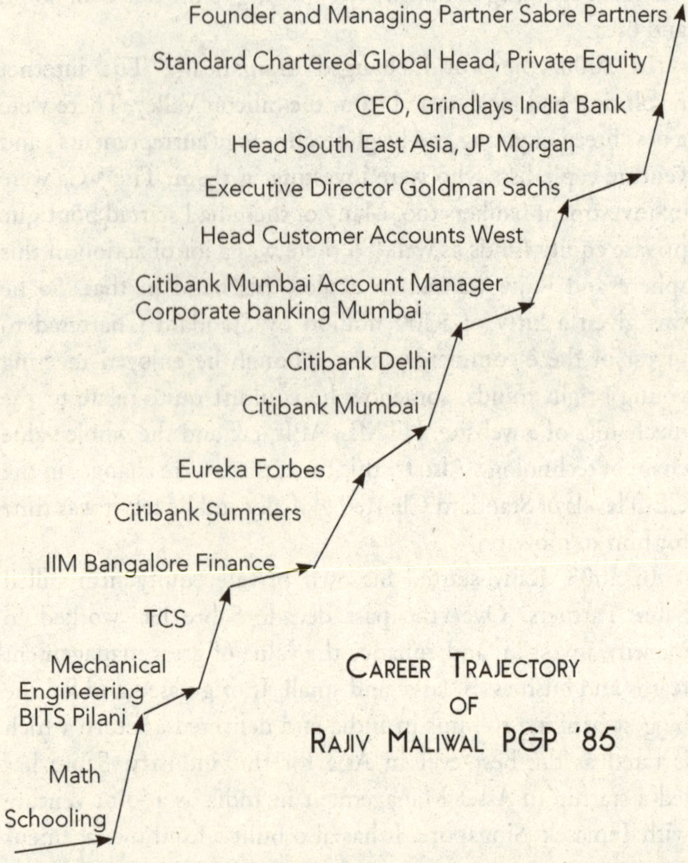


Career Trajectory of Rajiv Maliwal PGP '85

1. **Fortune favours those who prepare** – Rajiv's story clearly highlights the importance of preparation for career management. When I was a student, I read about the famous battle of Waterloo in which Duke Wellington and the allied armies defeated Napoleon Bonaparte. It was a historic battle that altered the course of world history and thus arose the famous quote, 'the battle of waterloo was won on the fields of Eton' which is used till today. This quote implies is that great preparation is required for things to go favourably. You can't wake up one fine morning and start climbing Mt Everest. It requires months of training and preparation. Every aspect of mountaineering has to be learnt and preparation to survive in extreme conditions must be done. So if you want to achieve something, you must prepare for it as well. Just like how Rajiv prepared really hard to get into Citibank, similarly one must not leave any stone unturned in preparing to take on one's goals.
2. **Don't rest on your laurels** – It's natural to feel good when one is rewarded for their efforts. Sometimes, we tend to measure our success in the form of designations or titles. We feel elated when we have fancy titles, get promoted or distinguished. While it helps to have titles and rewards that reflect well in your resume, it's important to remember that you need to constantly strive to do even better and be consistent. Don't rely on your past laurels beyond a point and don't let them get to your head. When you are hired to a top dream company, you are expected to deliver. Rajiv corroborates this by his own example. When he got through Goldman Sachs, they had very high expectations from him. Rajiv had to strive hard and prove his worth in this new company.

3. **Persevere. If the doors don't open, break the walls to go in** – Nothing can beat hard work and persistence. Sometimes, it's good to be obstinate and stubborn like a child when it comes to our career decisions. The traditional doors are not the only ways to get inside. There have to be other ways too. Rajiv proved this with the Citibank episode after his PGP program. He was not shortlisted for the final placement process and was disappointed. But he did not give up. He kept trying to find a way to get through Citibank and finally did. So don't give up. It's your dream and only you can make it happen. Persevere. The most common trait in leaders in any field is their dogged perseverance.

OPPORTUNITIES IN INVESTMENT BANK/PRIVATE EQUITY/VENTURE CAPITAL FIRMS

Investment banks help companies and governments issue securities, help investors purchase securities, manage financial assets, trade securities and provide financial advice. The top full service investment banks include Goldman Sachs, JP Morgan, and Morgan Stanley. Others are specialized firms called boutiques which might be oriented toward an industry vertical, M&A advisory, private equity, etc.

Venture capital or private equity firms are usually very lean firms without much hierarchy. Some of them are just two or three members in size. They usually prefer people with 3-4 year's experience in some startup, equity research, or consulting. Some VC companies are Accel Partners, Helion Venture Partners, Inventus, Nexus India Capital, Ojas Venture Partners, Sequoia Capital, and Venture East.

A student can start as an analyst or an associate in the following areas

Corporate finance, capital markets, mergers and acquisitions, project finance, trading, structured finance, derivatives, advisory, equity and fixed income research, international sales/emerging markets, public finance, retail brokerage/private client coverage/stockbroker, institutional sales, IT and systems, ratings analyst etc.

## Deeptha Khanna PGP '98

*Marketing Director Hair Care, Asia*

*Procter & Gamble*

Deeptha Chandrakumar Khanna graduated from the PGP programme of IIM Bangalore in 1998. She is currently the marketing director at P&G, a leading FMCG company, based out of Singapore and manages a portfolio that is about a billion dollars of revenue of hair care products like Pantene, Heads & Shoulders etc. She remembers that her childhood gave her a good platform to cope with different situations. Since her dad was in the airforce, she and her little sister would find themselves in a new school in a new city every two years. This made her more confident and helped her accommodate and acclimatize easily to any new environment. By the time she was in the 12$^{th}$ standard, she had changed nine schools. The one good thing was that all the schools were Kendriya Vidyalayas which had very similar structure, board, and people who were mostly from the defence forces. It gave her the chance to learn about various people, cultures and situations.

She was a bright student and since her grades were very good, she chose to study Science in the 10$^{th}$ standard. She was competitive when it came to academics and very active in the extracurricular activities of the school and the airforce community. Whenever there was an opportunity, Deeptha would be at the forefront of either participating in it or organizing it. There was one quality that made Deeptha stand out from other kids in her peer group—she was very sure about what she did not want to do. Her way of thinking was to eliminate what she didn't like or want, and then focus on what was left. This has helped her in all her career choices till today. In the 12th standard, she used this process to eliminate engineering and medicine for her career. She felt that since she liked being with people and at the centre of action, being an engineer or a doctor didn't seem anywhere close to the action she wanted in life. She was always the class monitor or someone who could communicate and get things done. Her skill of handling people and working with them stood out. But at that time, she really didn't know how to connect what she liked to do with what she wanted to do. There was not much guidance either from her social circles—majority of whom were in the defence.

Given that she didn't want to become an engineer or a doctor, she focussed on what remained of her options—science and law. She applied to the National Law School in Bangalore, cleared all stages except the final interview. That was a very disappointing episode but she took it in her stride and moved on. She then joined BSc in Math and Computers at St Francis College in Hyderabad. This was when she realized that she didn't connect to the idea of working with numbers and code. Though she remained a competitive student and was in the top 10 of her class, she felt bored with academics alone. At the same time, she continued to participate in as many extra-curricular activities as possible. She was a part of the organizing community of cultural fests and had participated in more than 60 such activities in less than three years. She knew every cultural fest of every college in the South through which she won many certificates and trophies. She wanted to participate and win. Her competitive drive was what pushed her to excel and made the journey worthwhile. Elocution, theater, poetry, you name a cultural activity, and Deeptha had done it. It finally dawned on her that she wanted to be a part of life and not just the office. So at the age of 20, she knew that her career has to incorporate a holistic set of everything that depicts life—and not just a designation in a company considered prestigious by society. She could have got any job in the IT sector in those days and done well there—but the IT sector is not a mirror of life, so she couldn't have been happy there. Her quest for finding meaning to her life lead her to find out about MBA and the IIMs. She found that an MBA programme provides the opportunity to have a holistic learning and she decided to walk that road. The IIMs were established as prestigious institutions by then and her competitive spirit had started to nudge her to prepare and write the CAT exam. Moreover, there was a CAT coaching institute which used to run classes in her college. So she went and sat for the classes. TIME a coaching institute was founded by two IIM alumni and she liked how they interacted with the students. They got various other alumni who were working in companies like HLL, McKinsey, Citibank and she got a chance to connect with the various facets of the MBA programme. Her training in Math and Statistics from her BSc background helped a lot as well. She sailed through the CAT by getting calls, and finally joined IIM Bangalore in 1996. This episode also gave a tremendous boost to her confidence which had taken a beating after the episode of NLS.

She gravitated towards subjects like consumer behaviour, marketing—anything to do with people, in contrast to subjects like finance and accounts at IIMB. She also met some seniors who now worked in marketing jobs in FMCG companies like HLL and P&G and realized that this was the kind of holistic job for which she was searching. It involves a lot of contact with people and also mirrors life. When the time came for her summer break, Deeptha had decided that she would try to take up an internship in a FMCG company. She was fascinated with how we all buy soaps, shampoos etc everyday but don't realize the amount of effort somebody would be putting in to make sure the customers relate to the products and buy them. The subjects of marketing gave her that theoretical knowledge and by then, she had completely eliminated finance related subjects and jobs from her life.

Given that she had narrowed down her career choice to only two companies—HLL and P&G, the chances for her getting into either for her internship were quite low as compared to her friends who had a wide variety to choose from. But she was determined. She told herself that she would leave no stone unturned. Everyone advised her to keep her options open but she was convinced that she would be able to make it. She applied only to these two companies and got offers from both. She was overjoyed and decided to join P&G. There were two reasons for it—one was that P&G was a choice that she had come after consulting with her seniors and peers, the ethos of the company gelled with what she thought she was as a person. P&G was the company that was widely quoted in Kotler—the bible of marketing. The second important reason was that P&G also gave final offers to the interns if they liked them. Given that she had already decided to be in a FMCG company for the rest of her life, she thought that this was her opportunity to convert the internship into a final offer as well.

She dove headlong into her studies and student affairs. By that time, the student elections were also coming up. The students have a very active SAC—Student Activity Centre which manages the entire gamut of their activities besides academics. This includes the cultural fests, sports, industry interaction and a variety of clubs focussed on the aspects of management like consulting, finance, marketing etc. Each club has its activity head and a team. The entire group elects a President who then becomes the face of the student body for the institute and gives direction to the SAC. There are budgets, sponsorships and an overall decorum that needs to be managed. There is lots of politics, fun and sometimes high drama too without which student life wouldn't be the same. Deeptha was quite a popular student but never in her wildest dreams had she thought of contesting for the post of the President. It was a thankless job, requiring a lot of people management between different groups and factions etc. And it was dominated by boys. One fine morning, she decided to apply for the position and contest. Everyone around her, friends, well wishers, juniors and faculty members were all surprised. Till now, IIMB had never had a woman student president. But all of this fuelled Deeptha's competitive spirit. She was popular, good with people, and wanted to be the first woman student president of SAC at IIMB. So she applied for the position and started campaigning. She had no group supporting her as it required lot of lobbying between groups.

Student politics is quite interesting. It combines a lot of factors—which engineering school you have come from, which state of India you're from, what language you speak etc. She had never factored in any of that. She just went with her best intention, and laid down her manifesto to the best of her ability. She went to every student in every room, handed out her manifesto, and slowly won them over. When the results came out, she was miles ahead of everyone. IIMB got its first woman student president in 1997 and Deeptha made history.

In the summer of 1997, she joined P&G as an intern. Her assignment was to figure out how to make owners of washing machines buy P&G brands—the washing power category. She totally loved this project and learnt a lot about how a company like P&G understands customer behaviours and evolves campaigns to reach out to them. After the internship was over, by May, the classes at IIMB started full swing by August, P&G

sent her a letter confirming her appointment after she finished her MBA. She was thrilled. Her dream had come true.

By the end of 1997, the prospects for an MBA didn't look very promising. Jobs were being cut and the economy worldwide was struggling. The student morale was quite down and most students feared for their future. She was one of the few lucky ones who had a confirmed job. So she started to work on every aspect of student needs—food in the mess, how to bid for courses and build up relationships with companies for placements. She learnt how to handle fellow students, groups, and manage the overall student politics. This was the time when she noticed how human behaviour changes with time. She saw a lot of people whom she felt were good and supportive and others who would backstab her to bring her down as the president. She saw how insecurity in people can make them do things which can be damaging and this helped her learn survival skills for the future. She was also thankful that she was in P&G because she really liked the culture of the company during her internship. People helped each other, didn't backstab each other and were genuinely supportive. The larger goal was important and everyone realized that if the goals are met, the insecurity can be managed better. P&G was not the best paymaster but she was convinced that a good work culture, good philosophy and ethos, and a long-term goal are more important than just a monthly pay.

With the P&G offer under her belt and having won the elections to become the first student president of the SAC, she now focussed on living life to the fullest. In the second year, she chose only those subjects that had classes from Mondays to Wednesdays. The remaining part of the week, she participated in competitions, extracurricular and cultural programmes of the city. She recalls that she and her team of three other batchmates won a case study competition from McKinsey and got a cash prize of ₹5000. This was a lot of money back then. So they decided to go to the swankiest restaurant in Bangalore then—Tandoor to blow it in style. The four of them dressed in their best clothes, pretending to be a well-travelled lot at Tandoor. Without even checking the menu, they ordered the finest food and wine; and were shocked when the bill came to be more than ₹10,000. Luckily one of them had a credit card and they paid up. Or else, it would be washing dishes all week at Tandoor to pay up the dues. They laughed their way back to campus and survived on whatever was available in the mess the rest of the month as they hadn't a penny left between them. In a series of many firsts, Deeptha organized the first all-night cultural programme with Spicmacay called Yamini and also took the students to Nrityagram and spent an entire day with Protima Bedi. She hopes that every student realizes how important college life is and cherishes this time as it will never come back. Deeptha also wrote a young adult novel that was published by Penguin. It is called *The year I turned 16*.

In 1998, she joined P&G in Mumbai and felt like a kid fresh out of school, armed with her bookish knowledge, in a land of grown-ups where you are expected to actually deliver. She was a quick learner, though. Her first assignment was with a famous brand for women's sanitary napkins called Whisper. She was the assistant brand manager and was responsible for the entire packaging of the product—the design, colour, layout wordings, proofing, etc. There was a new design getting launched and hence everything had to be done from scratch. She put in extra effort to make sure that things go without any problem. So she travelled to Aurangabad to make sure all the design, prints etc were perfect. She loved being in control and felt empowered. She also felt responsible that the company had put a lot of trust in her. Everything seemed fine in the factory and she saw them produce the first perfect print run. She felt satisfied and came back. The next morning, she got a call from the plant manager informing her that all the prints were done...but they had forgotten to add the bar code. Her blood froze. Without the bar code, there was no way they could ship the product as it is necessary for billing, tagging and the entire CRM systems. She asked how many were printed. The plant manager said—lakhs and lakhs. She put the phone down and walked up to her boss, informed him about the fiasco, and recommended that the entire loss was to be deducted from her salary. It was her responsibility to make sure that the print run went unaltered. She had failed. Her boss fell off his chair laughing and after a few minutes told her that he had never seen anyone think like her. He appreciated her loyalty to P&G but also explained to her what the right thing to do would be. He calmed her down and told her that everyone makes mistakes. She fell more deeply in love with P&G as she felt it had a culture that treated you with respect. With this episode, Deeptha decided that she would never leave P&G for anything else. Between 1998 and 2001, she was promoted to a regional brand manager and shifted to Singapore. In the meantime, she married her IIMB-classmate, and she was expecting her first child. She decided to take a year off to give time to her son.

In 2004, she returned to P&G and moved to Indonesia for an assignment. This was the time when the sales of P&G in this region were suffering quite badly. In a field like marketing, this is a delicious problem to explore and solve. Deeptha and her team did lot of research and instead of worrying about why the sales were going down, they started to study the Indonesian culture and how they used shampoos and soaps. The answer lay in celebrations and festivals. During the year, the most popular holiday season is called Libran (sometime during Eid). Most Indonesian people who lived in the city went back home to their villages or smaller towns to celebrate. The food sales would go up and most of the local distributors with shops that stacked up home needs, would obviously stack up more food to satisfy their needs and make more profits. So they removed or shoved the shampoos and soaps away from the most visible shelves of the shops and put food items there instead. Deeptha and her team brainstormed on this and explored ways on how they could convince the distributor or shopkeeper to stack more P&G products. They could always use brute force and their power. But it would be detrimental in the long run. So they started to think if they could have consumers buy more shampoos or soaps of P&G, just as they buy food during Libran? They noticed that these customers would stack foods in their suitcases and gift it to their families in the villages. The idea was to show to their village counterparts that 'I am from the city'. Food was one way to communicate this message. The other was the fashion statement of this person. And that was the ticket to their marketing campaign. They immediately got a campaign where they targeted this segment of customers and launched a slew of products to make them look good and sophisticated—hair colour, creams, lotions etc. The trick worked. Slowly the sales picked up and she and her team institutionalized a cultural paradigm to marketing in P&G.

Being in FMCG is like applying life every day. Imagine that whatever you work on is visible in every store of the street. You get a kick out of the fact that you see billboards everywhere of the product and the campaign that you worked on. When you walk in the stores and see people picking your product, you get an amazing thrill. One needs a tremendous sense of passion to observe people in this field. Which is why Deeptha loved it from day one—it was like living life at work. An example of this is her work for Whisper in Indonesia. The traditional Western approach of product position and promotion would not work in Asia. The girls in schools would not even discuss this topic.

They would use a cloth which would be very unhygienic. Deeptha and her team got to work this time using the social angle. They figured out that the reason the girls in the schools would not talk or use this product was because the decision of buying it was with the mother. So they designed a campaign where mothers and daughters were brought closer. It is the mother who would influence the daughter to use the sanitary napkin. In the campaign, they encouraged the daughter to give an appreciation letter/card to their mothers. This brought them together, made them to talk about this topic more openly and it helped everyone. Sales increased because now the focus was bringing the mothers and daughters together rather than positioning the product as just a sanitary napkin.

Deeptha is the marketing director at P&G today. She has two children now. Her relationship with P&G and the FMCG sector continues to be one big love affair that gets stronger every day.

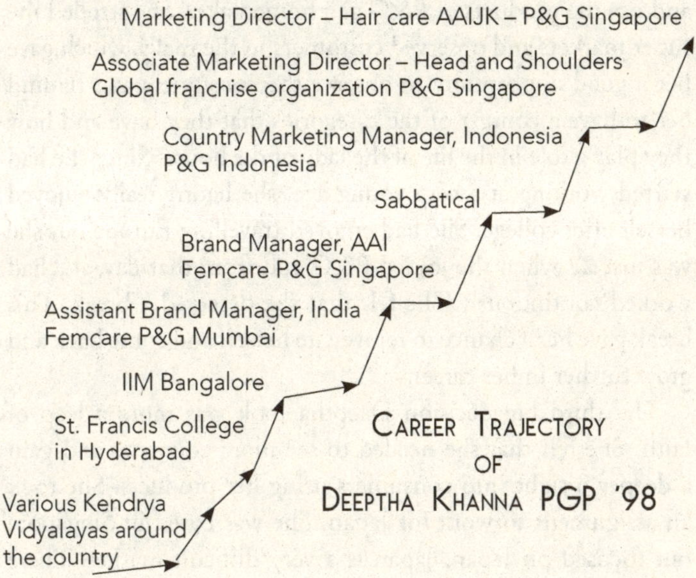


CAREER TRAJECTORY OF DEEPTHA KHANNA PGP '98

## Choices to the Top

For Deeptha, her career decisions were more about the location, in order to be with her husband Dinesh and keeping the family together. She had no reason to leave P&G. Growth and culture were the two reasons she stayed back. The company gave her every opportunity to see the world. So when she got the chance to move to Singapore, she took that up. The P&G office in Singapore is like a mini-world in one room. There are people from as many as 35 different countries. The amount she has bonded with them has really made her career and life richer.

The second big decision was to take a year off for her first born. It was not easy. But she wanted to give her first born all her time. So when Dinesh got an opportunity to go to Berlin for a year and come back, she thought that this was the perfect opportunity to give them time to strengthen their family. In hindsight, this one year gave her a platform to be a homemaker and use the products of P&G as a homemaker. She strolled the super markets and observed customers in the malls, which gave her a good opportunity to observe the consumers and remind her to have a context of the categories that they have and how they play a role in the life of the lady of the house. Since she had started working at a very young age, she hadn't really enjoyed herself after college. She had enjoyed travelling Europe but she was just 22 when she joined P&G and from that day, she had worked continuously. She felt that she deserved a break. This break gave her a chance to rejuvenate herself and come back and grow further in her career.

The third big decision Deeptha took was more a leap of faith. She felt that she needed to see more countries and gain a deeper insight into consumers using her products. She took an assignment to work for Japan. She was based in Singapore but focused on Japan. Japan is a very difficult market. There are language barriers, cultural barriers and whatever works in the world, doesn't apply in Japan and vice versa. So the first thing she decided to do was to move to Japan for a month on a holiday with her kids. She was all by herself. She took an apartment, camped there and experienced Japan not as a tourist but as a consumer. She observed the competition in their market, the buying habits of the Japanese consumers and their needs. This was a very risky assignment. Since by then she had become a very senior person at P&G. If she didn't show results, it would have adversely impacted her career. But Deeptha didn't let that deter her. She had faith in P&G's culture and her ability. She returned back after a month and this stint helped her with the marketing campaigns. She was able to relate to the problems and her strategy paid off. Overall, she didn't do too badly in this assignment. But the big lesson she learnt was that find a context and it will help find you find your larger purpose of life.

## Key Messages to Students

1. **Live life to the fullest** – According to Deeptha, the most important things for students today is to enjoy and live first. One of my favorite quotations in Kannada is 'Halla iddare kadle illa kadle iddare halla illa'. It's a very beautiful quote that translates to 'when I had a jaw, I didn't have nuts to eat. Now I have nuts to eat but don't have a jaw.' In every reunion that I see at IIMB, I always hear the alumni lament that they should have enjoyed their college days more. It was the same during my reunion as well. One of us commented something similar in a different way, 'Yaar, when we were in college, we had friends but no money to enjoy a party. Now we have the money but no friends.' Live your life to the fullest. Enjoy your friendships, your youth, and balance out the work effectively. Deeptha

participated in every cultural fest, travelled to different places with her friends, and had a whale of the time in her PGP programme. She also became the student president and worked really hard championing student causes while balancing the academics side as well. Companies too want students who are all-rounders.

2. **Be sincere** – Sincerity is a way of life for Deeptha. Whether it is being a leader at P&G, or the student president at IIMB, or a mother of two children at home—whatever she does, she does with utmost sincerity. She feels that it is the most important quality she looks for in others too. If one does their job sincerely, one can never go wrong. The best way to make career choices is to not club options as 'good' or 'bad'. Just make your choice and deliver with utmost sincerity. You will definitely get noticed and move up. Her first job in P&G was to get the new design and covers printed for her product. She could have done everything over phone, but she travelled to the factory just to make sure that the job was done well. This is the sense of responsibility and sincerity that has taken her places.

OPPORTUNITIES IN FMCG

Fast Moving Consumer Goods (FMCG) are all consumable items (other than groceries/pulses) that one needs to buy at regular intervals. These are items which are used daily, and so have a quick rate of consumption, and a high return. FMCG can broadly be categorized into three segments which are

- Household items like soaps, detergents, household accessories, etc

- Personal care items like shampoos, toothpaste, shaving products, etc
- Food and beverages like snacks, processed foods, tea, coffee, edible oils, soft drinks etc

Global leaders in the FMCG segment are Nestlé, ITC, Hindustan Unilever Limited, Reckitt Benckiser, Procter & Gamble, Coca-Cola, Carlsberg, Kleenex, General Mills, Pepsi, Gillette etc.

Working in the FMCG sector gives you the chance to be a part of some global success stories and influence the way consumers shop for products. You will need to have a creative bend of mind to think of innovative ways to differentiate your brand from the numerous others that meet the same need of the consumer. While there are various departments one can work in the FMCG companies just like any other company e.g. sales, R&D, product development, IT, finance, supply chain etc, these companies require more talented and creative managers in their marketing department. That's where the core understanding of their customers is and they use this to create products and plans around it.

Some jobs in the marketing department are as brand managers, marketing managers, market research managers and many more who liaison with advertising companies, media companies etc. Most FMCG firms are 'popular' for their induction programs which make the trainees go through the grind. The training program includes travelling to all the regions of India to understand the multi-cultural and multi-linguistic aspects of the country. It is focussed on selling, connecting with the consumer, and understanding the retail and distribution network.

## Vikash Daga PGP '00

*Partner McKinsey & Company*

VIKASH DAGA IS AN ALUMNUS of the batch of 2000. He is a partner with McKinsey & Company and is based in Delhi.

### The Formative Years

Vikash did his schooling from St Lawrence School in Kolkata. He did well academically and was a voracious reader, a habit that his mother had inculcated in him. He was also an avid quizzer. His father is an entrepreneur and had a factory that manufactured rollers that are used in bulk transport. Being from a business family in a city which is celebrated for the top quality chartered accountants and Commerce graduates it produces, Vikash got bitten by the commerce bug early on. From childhood he made his choices and was firm about them. When he was in Class 10$^{th}$, he started helping his dad with all the preparation in responding to tenders from various government manufacturing offices. He started enjoying finance and numbers and could do costing that was required to be filled into a tender. This gave him a first-hand exposure to the world of business. Many of his friends too came from similar families and when the time came for him to choose a subject; he was naturally inclined towards Commerce and BCom. At the age of 17, he was very clear that he would choose a life of business as opposed to other tracks of education that led him elsewhere. This quality of making good decisions in short time is a quality that has helped Vikash all along.

From St Lawrence, Vikash entered the prestigious St Xavier's for his BCom honours in 1994. One of the biggest advantages of being in St Xavier's was that he was studying what he liked and could also continue his articleship for CA simultaneously. The classes were from 6 am to 9 am in the morning. The entire day was then left for articleship. So Vikash enrolled in the articleship programme at a CA firm where he would do the basic work—balance accounts, make tax returns, do audits and the usual grinding work of account management. He did this for two years and realized that this work was too limited for him to do his whole life. He had many seniors before him who had become CAs and were very well known now. However, Vikash knew that he was meant to sail different seas. He quickly decided that he would not do CA beyond the articleship and began to consult his seniors for options.

Joining his father's business was an option he carefully considered. One day, his father asked him to travel to Jamshedpur to meet a client and submit the tender. It was then he actually saw that in the entire value chain of manufacturing, the part produced by his company was a very small and insignificant contribution. The company treated that part as a 'spare'. It was highly commoditized and anyone who had a small capital, a space to put a machine, could produce it in no time. The entire market was heavily fragmented and highly dependent on who gave the parts at the least cost. The world of sales was not simple and straightforward either. He discussed with his dad about growing the business to making more parts that were in demand but that required a lot of capital. In those days, the policies were not easy, private equity was a concept taught in books and applied in the Western world. So given the constraints, Vikash quickly realized that this path may not be viable for his ambitions of having a broader perspective in business at that time. 'I have narrowed down my choices wherever I have gone,' says Vikash. The faster you bring clarity in your choices, the easier the decision making becomes.

He had two roads in front of him. One was CFA which he felt was more ingrained in the world of accounts. The other was MBA. When he was in the final year of BCom honours, all his batchmates who had signed for BCom (which is a year shorter), started to write the CAT exam. He enquired further and got to know that there is an MBA programme of repute offered by the IIMs. Many alumni of St Xavier's had enrolled there and were doing quite well in the corporate world in a variety of roles of banking, finance, supply chain, and consulting. He also found out about the GMAT but he was never enamoured by the West. He felt that India was the country he belonged to and this is the place where he should study and work. He worked hard and wrote the CAT in 1997. He got a call from IIM Bangalore, and as was destined, joined the class of 1998-2000 of the PGP programme.

The first three terms at IIM Bangalore went past like a breeze. He was one of the toppers of the class all throughout. His knowledge of commerce and finance were his strength and he sailed through academics with flying colours. And then, something wonderful happened. He got introduced to a subject called Economics which opened his view on how the world of business really worked. His teachers from the economics department fuelled his hunger to learn more both on macro and micro economics. He started reading the available cases and literature, spoke to the professors and realized the importance of this subject to shape the future. But he also knew that he was less inclined on the academic side of economics. He was more interested in its practical applications to the world of business. His professors advised him to consider a job in consulting firms where he could best apply the theory he had learned in the class. This was the first time Vikash seriously explored the phrase 'consulting job'. In those days, there were few consulting companies who used to come for final placements. The most popular one was an American boutique consulting firm, which would place the candidate in New York on a 6-figure salary, probably the highest in India. But money didn't motivate Vikash. His parents and upbringing had made sure that money was never a deciding factor when it came to work. What were important to him were the impact and the learning that came with the work. He didn't want to leave India, either. So he asked about other companies and one of his seniors suggested he explore the opportunity with McKinsey and Company.

By then, the studies were keeping him more involved at IIMB and Vikash didn't have time to research that suggestion further. It was time to prepare for summer placements. He didn't really plan that much and told himself that any good company that offered work in finance was good enough for him to join. Since his academic record was so strong, he knew that he would be eligible to apply to any top company that came in. He had to think through the following choices—finance and banking (investment banks).

In those days, consulting companies didn't come for summer recruitment. Most of Vikash's batchmates thought that he would get into finance or a banking company. But Vikash didn't let perceptions and social pressures bother him. He took the summers quite lightly, got shortlisted in HUL in their finance and supply chain department, and said yes to the offer. He had a very high regard for HUL as a company and felt that he had won the lottery. Plus the person who came down for the interview was a very senior executive of the company. Vikash was very impressed by his talk and his vision. Somehow, this ability to make decisions on gut instinct have been very important to Vikash. He says that beyond a point, you shouldn't let perceptions cloud your thinking. He was very keen to get through an international bank which was offering an internship in London in their trading office. But he was not offered that position. In hindsight, this was a blessing in disguise as you'll see later in the chapter.

Vikash was delighted to get into HUL in April of 1999 for his internship. He spent a month at the head office in Mumbai followed by a month at a subsidiary company of HUL in Kolkata. He worked in their supply chain department and did cost allocations. His mind was quite open to learning and he was not too keen to impress them so much that they give him a job offer—something that most students would do. His work was so greatly appreciated that HUL did offer him a pre-placement offer at the end of his internship. He felt very honoured but also told HUL very clearly that his heart was on the consulting space. This quality of being honest and sticking to his guns has helped Vikash till now.

When he joined back in the 4$^{th}$ term of IIMB after the summer, he took up electives in marketing. Though, he knew that if he had to take up a consulting job, these subjects won't really help him. But Vikash was keen to learn this discipline for his self-growth. He feels that no learning is useless. It always comes in handy as we'll see later in the chapter.

One of the best features of the PGP programme at IIM Bangalore is the student exchange programme. Vikash applied to a school in Germany and did his 5$^{th}$ term there. This episode was the turning point in his life. In three months, Vikash saw a new world. He met professors and students from Germany and many other parts of the world. His project was a study on the emergence of Euro and the impact to the older currencies. He applied economic theories and learnt about operational and mathematical modelling to come to some conclusions. He loved every moment of this. He made friends with many students and since he was a vegetarian, he learned to cook for himself. He cherishes most of the friendships he made in those three months till today. The education system of most top universities outside India is very different. There was a lot of time for him to learn and research about his dream of a consulting job. He had a group of three friends with him for this project. They would discuss career choices in evenings, introspect and they all felt that given their love for the world of economics, finance and the fire to do bigger projects that impact policy, companies and the future, the consulting world would be apt for them.

He read the book *The McKinsey Way* during this period and was convinced that this is the place he wanted to be for the rest of his life. The internet had just opened up many possibilities and he used it to read more on the work McKinsey did. That year, McKinsey had just announced a report on the Indian IT/ITES/BPO sector. That report was the crowning accomplishment by a small team from McKinsey who did some cutting edge work on the future of this sector in India. NASSCOM was one of the partners as well. This was exactly the kind of work that excited Vikash. The more he researched about the company and the work they did, the firmer he became in his resolve that he will try his best to be a part of this company.

He had a senior who had got placed in McKinsey the year before. He traced his email id and wrote to him because he wanted more clarity on the boutique consulting firm vs McKinsey. The senior responded very crisply, 'You should join the boutique consulting firm only if you are looking for an entry into the USA'. Vikash read the response and felt happy that his gut feeling was right. With that last doubt eliminated, Vikash started preparing for his final placement process. Vikash also participated in a competition and won an opportunity to spend a week on the trading floor of a global investment bank. However, Vikash did not enjoy the experience and further reinforced the choice of consulting as a career.

In early 2000, Vikash came back to IIMB. He had a PPO from HUL which was good but he was clear on a future with McKinsey. His academic record was surely going to get him shortlisted for the interview. He consulted his professors and few seniors for the interview. Besides this, he was very calm about the whole preparation. The campus interviews started. He was selected by McKinsey after an intense round of interviews. He was delighted to make it to the best consulting company in the world.

## The Rising Star

In June 2000, he joined McKinsey as a junior associate. He was open to anything and was put on an IT services study with the same team that had published the IT/BPO services report he had read the previous year. At McKinsey, there is a very strong culture of apprenticeship. The seniors take the juniors as apprentices and teach them the art and science of consulting.

In McKinsey, life changes and you have to continuously keep upgrading your skills. You join as a Junior Associate and then move on to become Associate, Engagement Manager, Associate Partner and then a Partner to finally a Director. The culture of the company fostered learning and thinking out of the box.

Vikash got opportunities to work with the top IT and BPO companies of India. In a year, a consultant can do variety of roles—first as a researcher to dig through the problem, use management principles to come with a proposed solution, and then demonstrate that this solution will bring results.

When I asked Vikash about his future career plans and how he sees the next five years, he says that he is enjoying what he is doing as of now and doesn't really plan too much. His role is to build clients for the firm and create opportunity for others in the company to grow. Outside the firm, he has other goals. His family needs him more than ever and he has to strike the right balance.

## Choices to the Top

1. **Deciding to let go of CA and getting into IIMB** – Vikash feels that in hindsight, the decision to let go of CA and try for an MBA was not easy. The world of accountancy was his comfort zone. He could have done very well there. But he chose to try the MBA world because he knew that he wanted a broader approach towards life and career as opposed to a narrow one that the CA world offered. And that has paid off now.
2. **Getting into McKinsey and not investment banking** – In the first year at IIMB, Vikash was quite convinced that he would suit a consulting role better than a finance one. The experience on the trading floor of a global investment bank reinforced his beliefs on where he will fit better. His ability to follow his gut paid off really well.

## Flipside

1. **Prioritizing work over his family** – Vikash was really enjoying working with his clients but very soon realized that one can never get everything. So in pursuit of work, he feels that he ignored his family. There was a time he had three clients from three different cities. This took a toll on his lifestyle and family. But he quickly learnt from his mistakes and now balances between the two as much as possible.

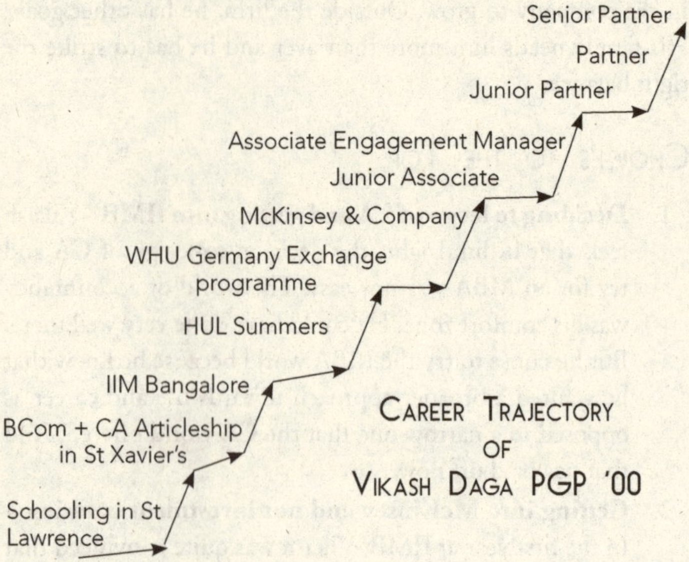


## KEY MESSAGES TO STUDENTS

1. **Build on your strengths** – Vikash says that the best way to build your career is to play to your strengths. Avoid trying to be someone you are not. If you are good at something, use that as a foundation to build your career. Pick few subjects that excite you and you know you are good at. Just because someone says that consultancy or I banks are hot, don't believe that. If you really like economics, finance and are patient to work on projects that are long, then look at a consulting role. Money is important but not a criterion on which you should base your final decision. Even if you do take a job that is not built on your strengths, very soon you will either get bored or your colleagues will figure out that you are not cut out for it. So either way, you will end up in a poor

light. Instead, choose a career that is to your strengths, prove yourself, and move up the ladder with time.

2. **Never underestimate the value of apprenticeship** – Exposure and apprenticeship are key to success, says Vikash. In the seventies and eighties, apprenticeship was considered very important for grooming future managers. Vikash feels that it is a much needed programme for students now as well. Colleges and students should find a seniors and experienced members in the corporate world—could be alumni, and use this connection to pass down best practices to the next generation. It has two advantages. One, the apprentice gets to learn and emulate a key learning from the senior that is useful for him in the industry and two it builds relations for life. This is not like a mentoring programme where things are very informal and depend on sharing experiences. This is a much more formal programme based on skills. In the olden days, this was the only way good artisans would pass their skills to the next generation. The apprentice would observe the master, get trained and then carry the tradition forward.

OPPORTUNITIES IN CONSULTING

You start as an associate and climb up the ladder to be a partner. The intermediate roles are designated by different names in different organizations. The way to grow in a consulting organization is to be an expert in your chosen field. As a result you will also know the interface of your area of expertise with the other business areas.

Many consulting firms are organized in a matrix structure, where one 'axis' describes a business function or type of consulting—for example, strategy, operations, technology, executive leadership, process improvement, talent management, sales, etc. The second axis is an industry focus—for example, oil and gas, retail, automotive. Together, these form a matrix, with consultants occupying one or more 'cells' in the matrix. For example, one consultant may specialize in operations for the retail industry, and another may focus on process improvement in the downstream oil and gas industry.

Some of top management consulting firms are—McKinsey and Company, Booz Hamilton, BCG, Bain and Company, and AT Kearney. Nowadays, there are many alumni consulting companies that have started their own boutique consulting companies too. Most consulting firms mandate a management degree; else you would need to be a doctorate or an expert in your field.

# Top Principles for a Good Career

Now that you have gone through stories of ten alumni who started like any other 20-year-old into the corporate world, I would like to highlight some of the common themes that are evident from their career trajectory. These themes can also be called best practices for career management. In most of my meetings with my friends in the corporate world and alumni from various other colleges of the world, I think the patterns that emerge out from good careers are very similar. Surprisingly, all these themes correspond to merely common sense but unfortunately are not applied very commonly. Those who apply these career management principles tend do well overall as compared to the others.

## Treat Career as a Marathon and not a 100-metre Dash

Though a marathon and a 100-metre dash have one thing in common—running, they both are meant for entirely different purposes and people. A 100-metre dash requires a person to train and strive to finish the 100 metres as fast as possible. The high of this race comes from speed. Every ounce of energy in the person is consumed to propel his body towards the finish line. Once this happens, the person is completely exhausted and cannot take part in another race after that. He has to take a break, train again, and apply the same method to get better and better at just one aspect—speed.

A marathon is totally different. It has various elements to the entire run—terrain, stamina, energy conservation, overcoming pain and cramps, mental power, ambience, audience, journey, speed, and the destination. So, a runner has to think very differently. He may be a 100-metre champion but he cannot apply the same method in a marathon. The most important difference between the two is that in 100-metre dash, the destination and reaching there in the shortest time is very important. But in a marathon, that isn't the case. The ability of a runner to conserve energy throughout the run, balance all terrains, enjoy the journey is of more importance than reaching the destination as fast as possible.

How does this become a best practice in career management? It's quite simple actually. A student thinking that getting a job out of campus is a 100-metre dash will invest all his time and energy on that goal. But that is just the first step. If he changes his mindset and treats his career as a marathon, then he will plan things more holistically, calibrate his energy accordingly, enjoy the journey, and take one step at a time to come closer to his destination. Just like a marathon, career has a terrain which is neither straight nor easy. It has ups and downs, climbs and falls. So students must learn to conserve their energy as they tread this terrain. Getting a job is just a milestone in this journey. The student should wear a long-term thinking hat at all times for a better career. Just as in the case of a marathon, it is important to take a break and catch your breath when you feel exhausted. A break rejuvenates you and you can resume the run with new energy.

An average adult has a career span of about forty years. The official retirement age is about 65 now. And I have many alumni friends who are showing no signs of slowing down at that age either. Not only in the case of IIMB alumni, I can share many examples from real life too where age has not been a challenge when it comes to career.The ISKCON movement was founded by Shri Abhay Charan De when he was 69 years of age. Before that, he translated the Bhagvad Gita for more than 10 years and before that he had a business in Kolkata. The ISKCON movement now is a force that does some excellent work worldwide—the most famous being feeding 15 lakh children everyday in the mid-day meal scheme that helps literacy as well. Another famous example is that of Mr Narayana Murthy who has joined Infosys again as its executive chairman. He is 66 and shows no sign of slowing down. If one has an active mind and a healthy body; I see no reason for that person to not etch a new curve in his career trajectory.

## Avoid Analysis Paralysis. Start Somewhere

If you ask anyone who has spent more than ten years in the corporate world, 'Did you plan to be here in this job 10 years ago?' I bet you that the answer would be, 'No'. It's only understandable that they say so. We all are mortals. We can't predict the future. We have no control over the world. The only thing we do have in our hands are our own actions which stem from our own decision. In all the stories in this book, a clear theme that stands out from the alumni's career paths is their ability of 'doing' rather than 'planning' beyond a point. One can really spend hours pondering and making plans on a comfy couch. But plans are just paper or thoughts in our mind that will change when implemented because the realities of the world will alter the scenario every minute forcing your plans to change. To strengthen your career's foundation, the more time you spend 'doing' things, the richer your career path will become. A summer internship programme, an apprenticeship, a degree/certificate course are all excellent pathways for students to go out and 'do' things. You can learn so much in just a day by working in that company than you will ever learn in a month by reading and thinking about it. Bottom-line, go out and do something. The more you plan, think and mull over your ideas, the more confused you will be. Remember the good old wisdom 'an empty mind is a devil's workshop'? So make sure your mind is always occupied with some activity that doesn't let the devil to hole in.

## Be the Best Rat in the Rat Race

When I was a young boy studying in Class $12^{th}$, preparing for my entrance exam, one of my father's friends came down to visit us. He was a man of few words, had serious health issues but was full of life. As part of being good host, I took him to the terrace of our house to show him the beautiful Umaid Palace of Jodhpur at a distance. As we looked on, he asked me about my future plans. Well, who at that age could answer that sensibly? So I mumbled some garbage and I now realize that when an adult asks this question to a young adult, its more to set the stage for the 'gyan' that is going to be spewed. I personally enjoy these gyan sessions. So I listened to him. I can never forget what he said to me that day. He said, 'Rakesh, do you know the second man who went to the moon?' I said, 'No, but I know who the first was.' He exclaimed, 'Exactly! The world doesn't care for #2.' The lesson hit its mark. I don't know why, but I knew that I had to do my best in my exams and be the best. This feeling of giving your best is very important in today's world. The world is highly competitive. Whether you love it or hate it, you will have to be a part of the rat race. No one can really avoid it. So give this race your best. Don't let mediocrity set in. Whatever work is given to you, do it by giving your 100 percent and make sure it is completed to the satisfaction of whoever has set the task for you.

## The 10,000 Hour Rule

One of the biggest 'Aha!' moments for me when I was writing this book was that one needs to spend years at an organization for his career to get a firm grounding. This was also corroborated by all the ten stories narrated in this book. In fact, a common theme that appears throughout *Outliers* by Malcolm Gladwell is the '10,000-Hour Rule', based on a study by Anders Ericsson. Gladwell claims that greatness requires enormous time, using the source of The Beatles' musical talents and Bill Gates', who founded Microsoft, as examples. The Beatles performed live in Hamburg, Germany over 1,200 times from 1960 to 1964, amassing more than 10,000 hours of playing time, therefore meeting the 10,000-Hour Rule. Gladwell asserts that all the time The Beatles spent performing it shaped their talent; and quotes Beatles' biographer Philip Norman as saying, 'So by the time they returned to England from Hamburg, Germany, 'they sounded like no one else. It was the making of them.' Gates met the 10,000-Hour Rule when he gained access to a high school computer in 1968 at the age of 13, and spent 10,000 hours programming on it. 10,000 hours roughly translates to about five years (assuming 1 year is 52 man weeks and 1 man week is 40 hours as defined by corporate guidelines). Recent trends in the markets show that the majority of students leave their first jobs within two years or less. Many students always ask 'what is my future employability options after two years from this job' as a way to decide their job. So it seems that before the students even enter their job, they weigh the options of getting into the next one. Now, I don't have evidence to suggest that if you change jobs in less than five years, you will fail. But this is what all my conversations with successful alumni suggests and what research by famous psychologists points at—'spend 10,000 hours or more'.

## Manage Your Boss Well

It is said that one cannot choose one's parents or bosses. Here's the bitter truth of your career—at no point of your career, you can ever have a situation where you don't have a boss. Let me say that again differently—you will ALWAYS have a boss to report to. Even if you become CEO of the world's biggest company, you will report to a board or the shareholders or the customers. You will have a lot more power for sure, but you will still have somebody above you. So, get this fact behind you and start to manage your bosses. They are regular human beings. They want to be successful in life too. Every relationship requires effort from both sides to make it work. Make sure that you put your best foot forward when it comes to your boss. Once you start making him successful, you will be amazed to see how much support he gives you. It's quite simple—if you have a great guy in your team, would you limit him with shackles or give him free reign to take you all higher? Even if your boss is from a completely different education background, e.g. you are an MBA and your boss is not, please remember that he is your boss. He must have done something better than you which has landed him where he is. I don't mean that you have to 'suck up' to your boss. There is a fine line between managing your boss and being the 'yes man' always. A good practice to move up the career ladder is to make your boss redundant every six months. Many good companies encourage this philosophy as it keeps everyone on their toes and ensures that the boss works hard as well to move up and make her boss redundant. Your boss is the first ticket to your success—don't forget that. Stop believing newspapers which quote the most clichéd HR statement, 'People don't change jobs; they change managers.' My view is that when people change managers without trying harder and as an easy exit, they lose an opportunity and have to start all over again.

## Survival of the Fittest

Remember the famous Darwinian theory of 'Survival of the fittest' that explained how certain species adapt themselves to the changes in nature and are better prepared to survive? Well, the same law applies to the corporate world too. Everyone is armed with a degree from some college. However, only those who adapt themselves and are fit will survive. The corporate world has its own norms and functioning, and it changes dynamically with time. So you need to be better prepared, arm yourself with newer skills and upgrade your knowledge, to survive the winds of change. Andy Grove calls this phenomenon 'paranoia'. He has written a wonderful book on it—*Only the Paranoid Survive.* He argues that even if you are a king and own a mountain, never rest on your laurels. Be paranoid that someone is lurking in the bushes and will take your place. So strive hard to maintain your position. In my talks with alumni, I found that every 10 years or so, they would sign up for a new skill or a course in some educational university, or with a professional agency. It could be a new spoken language too. As mentioned earlier, career is a marathon. So make sure you remain fit to run this marathon. Only those who are fit will make it to the finish line.

## What Got You Here Won't Get You There

The title above is also a very famous book by Marshall Goldsmith. This statement is quite self-explanatory. Let me put it into context. There was once a very famous Bollywood actor. He enjoyed such notorious fame in India that audiences would queue up in front of the cinema halls a night before to get tickets to see his movies. Many homes had his photo in place of gods and he was worshipped. He had everything one could dream of—power, fame, money, and a sound career. During every

Filmfare awards, he would sweep the most number of awards. But he was very unhappy. He felt like a big fish in a small pond. He wanted to enter into the global movie circuit—Hollywood and experience the glittering Oscar night someday. He dreamed of being the first Indian actor to have ever held an Oscar in his hands. So he spoke to few of his friends in Hollywood and got an offer to work with a world famous director. The movie was a big budget one and his role was not of the protagonist but that of a side kick. Our man was confident, thought that his time would come. After all, he had entered Bollywood in exactly the same style—with a small role and then slowly made his presence felt to where he was then before coming to Hollywood. His first day at the sets, he was given a script to read and a place to sit. He was shocked. This was not how he was used to being treated. So he threw a tantrum. His agents calmed him down and explained that things are different in Hollywood and that he had to fit in. So he tried to fit in. He gave his best to the role, and the movie bombed at the box office. His role went completely unnoticed. Even his fans back home didn't like the movie. He was severely criticized and he learnt a very important lesson. He learnt that he might be a superstar in Bollywood but that is no guarantee that he would do well in Hollywood too.

The same story is applicable in the corporate world. You could be a star in your college fest, the go-to person in your class, and the darling of your friends. But this doesn't mean that when you enter a company, you will automatically enjoy the same success. Never treat your past successes as an indication of your future. Your past laurels are no more than a small stepping point for you to climb up. If you are not prepared or ready to take this step properly, you might lose your balance. I'll give you another example from my corporate days. I won't name the company or the person. There was this star vice president. He was like god—Steve Jobs kind of stuff. He knew the product inside out, charmed his audiences with his clarity and vision, and gave the company a completely new lifeline by his product mix. In fact, in just about two years, he changed the future of the company. He was a very good business head and many argued that he was now being groomed for the top job. But for the top job, one needs to also spend time in the dumps—which was the sales department. He reluctantly agreed. We all thought that he would use his Midas touch and turn that dump into a swanky 5-star lobby. Surprisingly, he was a disaster. He made it worse. The customers hated his 'I-know-what-I-am-doing' attitude and very soon, the margins dropped as the customers signed up for a competitor product instead of ours. He had no choice but to leave the company but I am sure he learnt his lesson. I am told that the next company he went to, he was much better prepared and did quite well.

## Stay Focussed

A career trajectory can never be a straight linear line. It is curvy. It will rise and fall. The ability to handle failures and move on is very important in managing careers. The most important part is to stay focussed on your objective. I was reading the story of Ang Lee—the director of Oscar winning *Brokeback Mountain* and the recent *Life of Pi*. One of the journalists who had interviewed Lee in 1993 wrote a very heartwarming blog on his success and titled it quite aptly, 'Ang Lee and the uncertainty of success'. I am quoting few sentences from the author Jeff J. Lin written in 1993.

*From age 30 to 36, Lee's living in an apartment in White Plains, NY trying to get something—anything—going, while his wife Jane supports the family of four (they also had two young children) on her modest salary as a microbiologist. He spends every day at home, working on scripts, raising the kids, doing the cooking.*

*That's a six-year span — six years! — filled with dashed hopes and disappointments. 'There was nothing,' he told the New York Times. 'I sent in script after script. Most were turned down. Then there would be interest, I'd rewrite, hurry up, turn it in and wait weeks and weeks, just waiting. That was the toughest time for Jane and me. She didn't know what a film career was like and neither did I.' It got so discouraging that Lee reportedly contemplated learning computer science so he could find a job during this time, but was scolded by his wife when she found out, telling him to keep his focus. It wasn't until 1991 that Lee finally got a chance to helm his first movie, 'Pushing Hands', which wasn't even released in the US. But after 'Pushing Hands' came 'The Wedding Banquet', the film that would be his US breakout and net him a Best Foreign Picture nomination; two years later, 'Sense and Sensibility' would bring him into worldwide prominence; then a string of hits: 'Crouching Tiger, Hidden Dragon', 'Brokeback Mountain', and now 'Life of Pi' that have made him a common figure in the Oscar proceedings and the box-office charts ($576 million and 11 nominations for 'Life of Pi' alone).'*

Whenever I am going through a low patch in life due to some setback in my own career, I always think about the story of Dashrath Manjhi—also called the mountain man of India. He spent 22 years digging a mountain all by himself and finally gave the villagers a road that helped them save travel time by hours. The mountain stood in the way of his village and the town which had a hospital. The villagers had to go around the mountain to reach there which took many hours. Unfortunately, Dashrath Manjhi himself lost his wife in 1979; she needed medical help but couldn't reach the hospital in time and this drove him to dig the mountain and create the road through it on his own. Imagine the focus this man had. He would wake up every day for 22 years, dig the mountain, avoid the people who would make fun of him and just go on. The villagers thought that he was mad. But he didn't give up. And thanks to his efforts, when the road was completed, many lives were saved as they were able to reach the town faster. Sometimes it's a very humbling experience to see the difficulties others have faced in their lives, and how they still manage to smile and move on despite all odds. It takes tremendous amount of focus and grit in life to ignore the failures, learn from them, and still press on doggedly. In all the ten stories mentioned in this book, it was the sheer focus, persistence, and determination of each alumnus that brought them where they are today.

## Enjoy Your Career. Live it to the Maximum

The last theme that is very common amongst all successful alumni is that they believe that career is an integral part of life. You cannot separate it. It defines who you are and hence is a big part of your life. So enjoy it to the fullest. The corporate world is just like a school in many ways. You will make new friends, meet customers, travel the world, learn new things, and overall have a great time. How you live this life is completely dependent on your attitude. If you take it easy and go with the flow, you will have a great time. But if you treat it like an exam and are under pressure to perform all the time, you will end up resenting it all. I do know people who are very clear that for them a job or career is just to earn money to eat food. Many of them do various other things like have hobbies and enjoy them more than the career part. But I think they are just a handful and not something I personally connect with. I don't think I could enter my office thinking that I have to just pass time till 5 pm, earn my cheque and go back home to enjoy. I would get so bored sitting doing work that doesn't challenge me while in office and then go home and live my other life. It is not possible for me to divide my life into two parts as it's me who has to live it after all. So I choose to have an attitude where I wake up every morning, get ready with the feeling, 'I have to go to work and will have so much fun' and hope that this feeling stays till the day I die. The day I don't feel this way, I'll know that it is time to either find a new job or change myself. In either case, my objective is the same—that I will find a place for myself to enjoy and live to the fullest. Only then can I be most productive and create value for others.

# Building a Good Career

So how does one go about building a good career? Is it sheer luck or a well thought out effort? I see it as a very simple process which has multiple steps. Often, we don't even realize that we are following it as some of the steps are such routine part of how we think and live. I feel very strongly that every student should spend a lot of time preparing for this shift. Remember the different stages of a butterfly? Consider you are in the pupae stage as a student, protected and safe. Now you will become a butterfly, ready to unfurl your wings and fly. You will enter the unknown world, and make your own place. And you better prepare well for coming into this world.

When I was a kid, one of my icons was Wing Commander Rakesh Sharma who was the first Indian to go in a space flight. When I left the corporate world and joined IIM Bangalore in 2008 to build the alumni association and development office, I had the good fortune of meeting him in person at the institute. We had invited him to give a talk on the space programme and his experiences from that trip. One member in the audience asked him, 'Sir, why is the training programme of astronauts so strenuous and long?' Wing Commander Rakesh Sharma replied by citing a very simple analogy. He said that when we are trained to walk and run, there is an invisible force that helps us to coordinate the movements of the legs to touch the ground and lift back to give a running movement. That unseen force is gravity. So when we keep the foot on the ground, gravity relays to our brain exactly how much force is needed to lift the foot off the ground and move forward. But in space, gravity is non-existent. Our brains don't get to know how to control the muscles for basic movements as there is no feedback from the body to the brain. Hence the astronaut training programme is focussed to train this tiny organ of our body which we don't see but cannot do without—our brain. The astronauts are made to spend months in simulation chambers to get used to that scenario. And slowly, with practice and time, the brain starts to respond in such a situation and helps the astronaut do the important tasks for the mission in outer space.

I think seeking a career for a student today is no less challenging than an astronaut walking in space. I must emphasize the need for all students to prepare for this journey. Students may not be required to spend hours in anti-gravity chambers or underwater, but the key message here is—give some time and opportunity for your brain to get conditioned to enter that stage. Your brain is your control centre for this ship that you call your body. Your body is your temple. As you take care of your temple, take time to take care of your brain as well. If you have the time, watch a wonderful TED video by Dan Gilbert on how despite the best education and highly developed brains, when it comes to simple decision-making scenarios, we make mistakes that can be devastating.[1]

## The two commonly made mistakes are

1. **We make decisions based on what our mind remembers** – if you ask people whether an earthquake is deadlier to human life or asthma, chances are many of them will respond with earthquake. The reality is that more people

[1] http://www.ted.com/talks/dan_gilbert_researches_happiness.html

die of asthma than earthquakes every year. Now the respondents aren't foolish. They could be as smart as any of us—maybe toppers of their class. But when asked to pick between the two, their mind probably automatically refers to the last news flash in a paper or TV or Internet about a devastating earthquake. Nobody reads or reports asthma deaths as they are not newsworthy. Past data and episodes influence as well. This theory also helps understand the simple phenomenon 'Why people buy lottery tickets' and the answer is that they remember the smiling faces of the handful winners on TV. No one reports the millions of losers of the same lottery.

2. **We make decisions based on comparison** – When we compare one thing to another, the relative value of that entity changes the evaluation in our mind. Often, it can result in a poor outcome. The best example is that of you buying mangoes from the super market. You are walking down the fruit and vegetable section and see that the price of a kilo of mangoes is ₹100. But if you buy two kilos of mangoes, the price is ₹180 and you will save ₹20. Your mind immediately begins to compare. It also tells you that if you go to the local fruit market and pick the mangoes from a roadside fruit vendor, you might pay ₹150 and be able to save ₹50 for two kilos. So you decide to let the offer at the super market go, drive all the way to the local market, struggle to find parking, and waste enormous amount of time to save ₹50. At that point, all you care about is the ₹50 you're saving. Not the mangoes. If you add the time you spent wasting by not buying at the super market, cost of petrol, parking hassles—you probably paid only ₹150 from your pocket, but at least ₹30 on the rest that you don't account for. So you see

how the brain can play havoc on making simple decisions. Comparisons always take place anywhere we go and the more we compare, the more prone we are to making poorer choices.

If I use these examples above to the problem at hand – how students seek careers, I think I now understand why most students chase investment banking careers. That's because all newspapers report how well the jobs in investment banks pay. All students compare the salary first and glamour next. So even if you are a BSc in Math and Computers, if you get to choose between a job in Goldman Sachs IT department and an embedded systems programming role in Wipro, many students would choose Goldman Sachs because their mind recalls this name in connection to a high paying job and as compared to Wipro, they do pay very well. Chances are, this person, after joining the IT department of Goldman Sachs would realize he is a misfit and end up changing his job very soon. Instead, if this person just spends a little time to groom his brain to make the right decisions and by avoiding the traps of the mind, he could have saved his career from a dismal start.

## Seek and You Shall Find

### *Six steps to your dream job*

So what is the right approach for getting your dream career? Given below are the six steps I would like to propose after researching over this topic and meeting many alumni who have applied this to their own careers.

1. Minimize your constraints
2. Find out what excites you

3. Find the right job in the right company
4. Prepare and focus
5. Seek
6. Have a plan B

## Minimize Your Constraints

Earlier, I had highlighted 7 problems that students face in making career choices. They were

1. Parents dictating every move
2. Financial burdens
3. Social and peer pressure
4. Information gaps
5. Myths, biases, and prejudices
6. Hierarchical systems and pecking orders
7. Fear of failure

For the first step a student should rank them on a scale of 10, where 1 is the lowest level of problem and 10 the highest. You can mark them on the table similar to the one below. Don't think too much. Just pick whatever number that comes to mind that gives you a rough idea whether this particular item number is a small problem, medium problem, or a BIG problem.

| Problem faced by students | Scale (1-10) |
|---|---|
| Parents dictating every move | 9 |
| Financial burdens | 9 |
| Social and peer pressure | 5 |
| Information gaps | 1 |

| | |
|---|---|
| Myths, Biases and prejudices | 1 |
| Hierarchical systems and pecking orders | 1 |
| Fear of failure | 10 |

Let's say you filled the table as above. What this means is that you have a set of parents who dictate your every move, you are in serious financial burden, and you don't take too many risks. You do have a peer pressure but it is medium—not too high nor too low. Your parents, your loan (financial burden) and your inability to handle fear are defined as 'Constraints' for your decision-making system. You have only two ways to move forward. Either you **acknowledge** them and make your choices based on your constraints or find a way to **eliminate** them. To clarify, you have two scenarios now

Scenario 1 – Acknowledge your problems which means you accept them

Scenario 2 – Eliminate your problems which means you remove them

The more problems you eliminate, the freer you will be to make better choices. Now let's apply both scenarios to the one of the problems as listed in the table above: Parents dictating every move. If your parents are very rigid and follow 'it's my way or the highway', and you have no choice but to go with scenario 1, acknowledge it, and do what your parents think is best for you. But if you want to eliminate the problem, then I think you should think through the following options on dealing with this scenario

1. You take the highway or in simpler words, rebel against your parents like the guy does in the movie *Udaan.*

2. You talk to them, reason with them and have them buy in to your plans. Remember Kajol in DDLJ? She knows her dad (the scary Amrish Puri) won't let her go to the Eurail trip for a month. But she wakes up early in the morning, does puja, impresses him, and then pleads with him to say yes. And he does. Parents love you. It's just that they are afraid that something bad might happen to you. They need a transition training as well to let you become an adult.

Do the same exercise for the other problems. Let's take financial burden and define it—in this case, let's define it as the educational loan of say ₹10 lakh. If you have a poor financial background, and have no one in the family who can help, then acknowledge the situation, and take the load on your shoulders. If you want to eliminate the problem, you have the following options in front of you

1. Ask your parents or elder brother/sister, friends, spouse to pay off your loan or 'loan you a loan with no interest'. That way, at least the sword of the EMI will be off your neck.

Fear of failure is one of the most difficult of all fears to handle. it can strike at any age. And there is no easy way of removing this completely. Instead, there are ideas to handle or overcome it differently. So let's first define fear of failure. What is it exactly? I have heard some students say 'Sir, I don't want to end up like him' where 'him' is a fellow student who is doing very badly in his career. Also, we see movies or read examples in media on how someone takes a bad decision, loses his job, and then struggles for survival. One student recalled his mom saying, 'If you don't study hard, you will become a beggar on the street'. So let's picture that failure and understand it better. Some other answers are 'I will die of hunger' or 'the bank people will send goons and thrash me'. Fear has a face. Let's bring it out from the closet and look at it straight in the face. Now try and find what you can do to eliminate it. Fear has to be overcome. Don't let it sit there. Some simple ways for you to do so are as under

1. **Talk about it to your parents and friends** – The more you bring it out in the open, the more different perspectives you will get on how to deal with it. To give you one example of the fear mentioned above 'I will die of hunger…', just look around you. If you can find a single person who is hungry after having an educational background like you, then you have a right to be scared. But the fact is—you will *not* see a single person who is as educated as you are and hungry. Even the beggars on the street don't go hungry at all times. So most of the fears are just blocks in our minds. Fight them.
2. **A big reason of fear is insecurity** – There is only one way to fight it—believe in yourself and believe in God. Raise your spiritual awareness. You are in this world for a reason. There is a place for you. Just like how when you were a child and knew that your dad will take care of you, similarly, even now, your spiritual dad is always there to take care of you. So don't be afraid. This belief might take time to take root in you. But if you get a chance, read the Gita. There is a reason why that book, written 5000 years ago, is still relevant today.

Eliminating peer pressure and the other three problems namely information gaps, myths, and hierarchical systems are very easy. All you need is a good mentor who can help you with ideas on getting over all of these problems. Here is what I do to eliminate them

1. **Peer pressure** – I just stop talking to my friends and informing them about my plans. It's my life. I see no reason to ask or share with anyone what my career plans are. I stop posting things on Facebook as well. And I stop looking at what others are doing. I pretty much isolate myself and make sure that the iron curtain doesn't let their opinions in. After all, the pressure comes when we listen to them. So stop listening to them. They are your friends and social circles. They are *not* your stakeholders that you need to keep happy. And if you lose them in this process, don't worry. It's probably good riddance and you will make new circles very soon.
2. **Information gaps** – talk to a senior who you can trust—a mentor, if you will. Spend more time researching the right information. For example if you want to know about the banking sector, identify three seniors through your alumni associations to talk to. Avoid getting biased with what you hear from them. Use your own judgement to make decisions and use the seniors as a sounding board. The next two ones are very interesting. They are actually connected to the other fears. If you can get rid of the peer pressure and other problems mentioned above, then these won't bother you at all.
3. **Myths and biases** – I think the ten alumni stories mentioned earlier shatter many of the myths and biases. Revisit them and just ignore this set of problems.
4. **Hierarchical system** – This problem is a deep rooted problem in one's upbringing, culture and surroundings. Exposure to the world is the best way to get over this problem. I recall that when I went to the US for the first time, I actually saw people taking pride in their work. No matter if you were a CEO or a janitor of the company,

both of them parked their cars in the same parking lot. The more you see the world and become a global citizen, the lesser this poses as a problem. And again, best is to ignore this and move on.

A simple tool to help you eliminate your problems. This is just an example of what I would do for my own.

| Problem faced by students | Scale (1-10) | Option | Action |
|---|---|---|---|
| Parents dictating every move | 9 | Eliminate | Talk to parents |
| Financial burdens | 9 | Eliminate | Take help from family |
| Social and peer pressure | 5 | Eliminate | Stop being in that circle |
| Information gaps | 1 | Eliminate | Get a mentor |
| Myths, Biases and prejudices | 1 | Eliminate | Ignore |
| Hierarchical systems and pecking orders | 1 | Eliminate | Ignore |
| Fear of failure | 10 | Eliminate | Fight your fears |

For some students, avoiding financial burdens may not be an option. So, in that case, the table might look as below.

| Problem faced by students | Scale (1-10) | Option | Action |
|---|---|---|---|
| Parents dictating every move | 9 | Eliminate | Talk to parents |
| Financial burdens | 9 | Acknowledge | |

| | | | |
|---|---|---|---|
| Social and peer pressure | 5 | Eliminate | Stop being in that circle |
| Information gaps | 1 | Eliminate | Get a mentor |
| Myths, Biases and prejudices | 1 | Eliminate | Ignore |
| Hierarchical systems and pecking orders | 1 | Eliminate | Ignore |
| Fear of failure | 10 | Eliminate | Fight your fears |

Now that we have dealt with some way of eliminating or minimizing our constraints, let's take the next step in building a good career.

## Find Out What Excites You

This step is a slightly tricky one. So if you don't have an answer for this, try and read this section to discover where your passion lies. Even after that, if you don't have a very concrete answer, don't worry. It's okay to not have an answer for this section at your age. I know of many people who are touching 40 and still are not sure what excites them. There is nothing wrong in saying 'I don't know' for this question.

Here are some ways to find an answer to this question

1. **Eliminate the things you clearly don't want in a future career** – This is pretty easy to do. Just list down few things that you will never do in your job or you don't like to do. This list can also have the things that bore you. Let's say you are an engineering graduate from the Mechanical branch. Make a table with the thing you don't like with an additional column that describes why you don't like

doing this. An example Karan filled below who is from Civil Engineering.

| Things Karan would not like to do in future career | Reason |
|---|---|
| Computers, Coding, Testing, IT | Boring |
| BPO, KPO | Doesn't sound challenging |
| Fixing bikes or cars | Am too qualified |
| Finance and numbers | Bad at math |

2. **What are your hobbies** – Things that energize you when you are bored. Again make a simple table as below. In the next column, just answer a Yes/No/Maybe to the question, 'Can you make this hobby a full time job and make money?'

| Some of Karan's hobbies | Full time job |
|---|---|
| Reading and watching movies | No |
| Eating and being with friends | No |
| Painting | Maybe (not sure) |
| Travelling | No |

3. What subjects in your course were your favourite or got you top marks. Do you like these subjects and can do a job based on them?

| Favourite subjects in engineering | Full time job |
|---|---|
| Thermodynamics | No |
| CAD/CAM | No (don't like computers) |
| Automobile engineering | Yes |
| Manufacturing systems | Yes |

4. **What do you think are your strengths** – This is a very clichéd question but nevertheless needs to be fleshed out. And the column next to it, think through why you think this is your strength. For example if you think that you are good with people, the why column should contain a proof that this is indeed a strength and not a CV building question you have asked your friends and pasted here. (PS: If you are expecting a question on weakness, it doesn't exist in my book. Just play to your strengths!) Below are Karan's strengths.

| Strengths | Proof (why?) |
|---|---|
| Very friendly and outgoing | Have 500 Facebook friends who I have met and know each one by name |
| Extracurricular activities | Won an award for designing a low cost 4-wheeler |
| Problem solver for my friends | My friends tell me that the only person they call when they are in trouble is me. I get things done. |
| English – spoken and written | My blog has 1000 followers. I MC events |

5. **Wild card question** – Who are your role models and why? For example, who is that person in this world you feel inspired by and feel 'I want to be like him/her'. And also answer why does this person inspire you or why do you want to be like him/her?

   Below are people who inspire Karan.

| My idol | Why |
|---|---|
| Bill Gates | Richest man |
| Mahatma Gandhi | Honesty |
| Anand Mahindra | Mahindra SUV |
| Steve Jobs | I phone |

After this exercise, if your answer is still 'I don't know', it's still okay. Don't worry. But if the answer is similar to above, then try and look for a pattern. If I look at the tables filled above, Karan may fit the manufacturing sector very well. Karan likes the mechanical subjects for automobile engineering, has good strengths that fit this (award that he won for designing the lost cost vehicle), and his idol is Anand Mahindra because he loves the Mahindra SUV. But don't force fit all this. Just paste these tables on your wall and let them sit for a while. It's okay to make changes and fine tune them with time. The whole idea is to come to a stage that answers 'Yes, this particular area excites me'.

## Find the Right Job in the Right Company

Assuming that step 2 above gave you a broad area which excites you or motivates you professionally, now is the time to dive deeper and do the following

1. **Research the sector** – Researching is an art and requires more than knowing www.google.com. Some good resources of finding about Indian companies are CII, Nasscom, Assocham and many more such official bodies affiliated to the Government of India. Each sector has its association details which will be available with the Ministry of Commerce. Broadly, look for answers to the following questions while researching

a. How old is this sector? What is the history; how it evolved over years? There are wonderful books written on the history of industrialization. Lap this up.

b. What are the various parts of the value chain in this sector? A value chain is defined as the various parts that connect the production to consumption aspects. For example, for the automobile sector, try and understand every aspect of how a car is made, its raw materials that go all the way down to metals, plastics, electronics, manpower to technology, operations and all the way up to retail stores.

2. **Research the company** – In each of the parts, what are the top five names of companies that are there today. Note down their websites and read about the company history, founders, profitability, competitors, media presence, current CXOs, investor views, trends from experts on this sector etc. Shortlist 3-5 companies that you like most.
3. **Research the jobs in these companies** – Now find out all the kinds of jobs available in these companies from available sources that you have—your alumni from school, colleges and social circles. LinkedIn is a great tool for cold calling people working in these companies and ask them about the various job opportunities, what they do in a given day, and how their career has progressed.
4. **Identify which jobs you would fit in** – Once you have a handle on the company and the kind of roles available, now see where you fit. If you are a fresh student from engineering, then you obviously don't fit the CXO category of jobs. Try and explore the entry level jobs—for engineers, usually called Graduate Engineer or Trainee Engineer.

5. **Read the job description** – This is the most important part. Make sure you read the job description carefully and that it relates to 'what you like to do'. Most of the time, the student stops at point number 2 above. So you may end up in the best company of the world but doing a job you don't like.
6. **Read the parameters that match your needs (salary, city, perks, quality of work etc)**

At the end of this step, you should have a very clear job in a particular company and a clear job description. Most importantly, you should like it and want it—and I mean badly.

## Prepare and Focus

Remember the story of Arjuna and the eye of the bird? I have mentioned this story earlier in this book. Let me refresh your memory. Guru Dronacharya was teaching archery to his disciples—the Pandava and Kaurava brothers. He took them to a place in the gurukul, pointed his finger to a tree about 100 metres away which had a wooden bird perched on the top. He challenged his disciples that the person who could pierce the eye of that bird would be called the 'best archer' in the world. Everyone except Arjuna failed. That's because only Arjuna was prepared and focussed. All he saw was the eye of the bird. So if you want to get that dream job, you must see only that. Nothing else. To apply for a job, there are some standard pre-defined steps that are needed as preparation.

1. **Focus** – First, take a printout of this job title and the company and paste it in front of your table or the wall or at a place which constantly reminds you about your goal. You must see the eye of the bird clearly at all times. Nothing else.

2. **Get shortlisted** – Sharpen your resume. Think about how you will convey in the resume that you are the best candidate to be shortlisted. A resume is a sales document. Be honest, don't sand bag information and make sure that you know every word of your resume by heart. Your LinkedIn profile should resonate with your resume. I will tell you why this is important. Say you get shortlisted and your resume says, 'Leave no stone unturned' by Euripides. If the recruiter asks you 'Who is Euripides', you better answer that well. So don't cut paste what your friends have done. Avoid clichéd sentences that sound like you will solve world hunger etc. Focus on what your reasons are to fit this role. Talk about your academic accomplishments especially in those subjects that fit the job profile. Sprinkle your human side a little—maybe the work you do for children, and a word or two on your hobbies like music etc. A resume is your first step into the corporate world. Please remember, it is a document that conveys who you are. So any word that is not honest might become your grave. I am told that as much as 30 percent of resumes are fake. Many students also fudge their academic qualifications, marks etc. Transparency is very important. If you don't believe me, look up the Yahoo ex-CEO Scott Thomson's story. You will find that he was fired because his resume had discrepancies.
3. **Find out what will be asked in the interview** – Ask your seniors who may have gone through a similar interview on what kind of questions you may want to prepare for. Do a dry run for as much of them as possible.
4. **Differentiate yourself** – When you look at your candidature, ask yourself, what gives me an edge over others from my own college of my kind of background. Just

like you, there will be at least 1000 more with the same degree, better marks, and similar offerings. What makes you different? Some ideas I can give you based on what I see my alumni doing are

a. Learn at least one new language besides Hindi, English, and your local language.
b. Write at least one academic paper (not blog) in a subject that you like and that fits the job/company/sector.
c. Do at least one extra apprenticeship or internship than the regular one from your college. Go sign up a project with a startup or an NGO. Work with them and learn something new that can add value to the company you want to work for.
d. Win at least one award in an area that you think you can do—sports, cultural, extra curriculars. And I don't mean an award like 'Best tie at the evening dinner' kind of award. Something visible and recognizable.
e. Any failed project—don't hesitate to talk about your failed projects and ideas if needed. I think a student who has started a small initiative, tried for six months, made a prototype, took it to market and then realized that it won't work is an excellent person to hire for any company. The idea here is that you can differentiate yourself based on this rich six-month learning that you got on your own that others might not have.
f. Bring at least one testimonial from a senior alumni or your industry mentor who is reasonably known.

5. **Invest in your personality** – Most students often underestimate the power of personality—the way you dress, the way you look and the way you make your first impression.

They see their seniors, buy exactly the same clothes to fit in and miss making the impressions. I have seen students spending at least ₹10,000 on good shoes, shirt, tie, and a suit but all terribly colour coordinated. They look like oversized penguins—black suits, dark shirts, jarring ties, belts with buckles that stand out or socks that haven't been changed since class 10th. (In one of my talks at a college, I noticed one student wearing a belt with a buckle that had 'Playboy' written on it. Another student wore a heavy black boots with white socks and dark trousers.) Sign up for a grooming course; learn how to greet, exchange cards, dress, stand, and walk and talk well etc. It will take you a long way. The college life was all about jeans, coolness and awesomeness. You could get away with a crumpled shirt or hair. But not now. The world is watching you now. So get ready to look and behave your best.

6. **Network** – This is one of the most undervalued skills in our culture. You have the whole world out there to go and network with. Meet your alumni. Go to conferences and trade conventions (students get free passes). Check out the events section everyday in the news and walk up to any activity that is professionally managed by a company. There are seminars, webinars and a whole lot of things happening out there. Collect as much business cards as you can and stay in touch with your contacts.

At the end of this step, you should feel 'I am ready' for this job.

## SEEK

You have prepared well. All you now see is the eye of the bird. So go ahead and shoot. Seek your dream. This is the D-day. Have faith in yourself and let the arrow go. Give it your best shot. Let your mind think of nothing else except this. Immerse yourself 100 percent into your goal. Here are some ideas on how to do this.

1. **Demonstrate your excitement about this job** – I don't mean fall at recruiters' feet and show desperation. There is a fine line between demonstrating excitement and showing desperation. Give a big smile when you meet them in the interview, thank them for giving you an opportunity, and be positive. A simple beaming smile can do wonders here.
2. **Answer to the best of your ability** – Many times, students feel that they have to answer every question. It's not true. If you don't know the answer to a question, smile and say 'I am sorry, I don't know', or 'I am not sure'. Its okay to say that. You are not expected to know everything in the world. But please don't faff around. Learn when to speak and when to listen.
3. **You can ask questions too** – An interview is a two-way street. So when you get a chance, ask them questions that you may have about the job, company, and its plans for the future. Don't hesitate to connect with the recruiter. After all, you now may become his future colleague and a friend for life. So stop behaving like a student. Behave like a grown up and a professional.
4. **Relax your mind** – Tell your mind that success or failure is an outcome. So don't lose your head for this job. Be prepared to hear 'no' from the recruiters. Relax your mind. If you miss this train, wait for the next one.

You have fulfilled your part. Now the real world dynamics will kick in and this is beyond your control. So sit back and relax for the results to come. The great poet Rumi, said 'What you seek is seeking you'.

## Have a Plan B

Sometimes, despite the best plans and preparations, things still don't happen. There could be various reasons for this and because of a variety of external factors. First find out where things went wrong. Here is a table that might be of help. The first column will help you listing down the reason. And the second is to find out whether it was you, or the external factor? Make a case study like the one below

| Reason of failure | External/You |
|---|---|
| The company's requirements changed — they realized that they can't hire anymore. Economic up/downturns do impact hiring | External |
| You did not do well in your interview, or maybe your resume didn't spell out your strengths clearly | You |
| There were better candidates than you | You |
| There were just few positions and though they liked you, they didn't have space to get you as well | External |

Find out why you didn't make it and make sure your approach is to learn from this episode to improve. Don't drown yourself in depression. We all have ups and downs. You have read ten stories and many of them talk about how they failed many times. The key here is to keep trying and have a Plan B. So here are some suggestions for your Plan B.

1. **Wait for some time and re-apply** – Before you do this, take the help from a mentor from that company on the

right time to re-apply. The best is to stay in touch with the person who recruited you.

2. **Apply to other companies in same sector with similar profile** – You have done your research well. You should have at least five more companies in that sector looking for a profile like yours. So please go back to step 3 above and follow for all companies.
3. **Fine tune your entire Seek Algorithm and go back to the drawing board** – Sometimes, we often make the same mistakes. So a good way to avoid them is to start afresh—from scratch. Recalibrate your goals, objectives and see if you end up in the place you like. But don't do it all the time. You cannot change who you are and what you like every day.
4. **Find a place to keep the metre running** – A short course to boost your skills, or an internship/apprenticeship programme are great ideas to get a place in the corporate world, keep the meter running and use that time to hone your candidature.
5. **Join a startup or a NGO** – Startups are wonderful breeding grounds to learn new things. They always need people who can get work done with minimal requirements. So are NGOs. Go ahead and work with them. Don't bother about salaries. First you will get to learn, your resume will also benefit and secondly, if the corporate sector doesn't work out, you can find a good place in these companies too. Many of them become very professional with time and you could be that early sapling which grows in the garden and very soon, becomes a leader within that space.
6. **Consult with your mentor** – This is where you really need a person to talk to. Your dad, elder sibling, senior alumni, friends—anyone who can pull you up from the dumps.

Be willing to share your feelings, use them as sounding boards. Remember—God is always there near you as your mentor. Don't hesitate to close your eyes and talk to him.

WHILE THE SEARCH IS ON, REMEMBER TO NEVER

1. Forward your resume to the whole world, especially alumni, without knowing them personally.
2. Judge a job just on the salary.

Double check those jobs that sound unconventional, for example 'Chief dreamer'. Focus on the Job description and not the title.

# In Parting

I GOT MY CAMPUS OFFER TO join Wipro Technologies and joined in July, 1997. I have truly tried to follow some of the advice I have mentioned in this book in managing my own career till now. when I was about to take the train from Jodhpur to go to Infosys, Bangalore in the summer of 1997, my mom gave me a sealed envelope. It said, 'Read it carefully, son.' I still have that letter and read it quite often. My parents are doctors and understand the world of medicine quite well. It amazes me that what my mom wrote in that piece of paper is true and relevant for everyone in managing our lives and career, not just for doctors, engineers, MBAs, or lawyers. The ten stories I shared with you also echo many of these points and I thought that it's only fitting that I share the letter with you all too.

Dear Son,

You are starting a new chapter in your life. Our good wishes and blessings are always with you. Although you are 21 years old and have matured but still there are some instructions/advice or whatever you feel from your parents which you must keep in your mind.

- Watch sunrise as frequently as possible
- Say 'thank you' a lot
- Treat everyone you meet as you want to be treated
- Live beneath your means

- Don't waste time learning the tricks of the trade; instead learn the trade
- Admit your mistakes. Be brave. Even if you are not, pretend to be. No one can tell the difference
- Never cheat. Learn to listen. Keep secrets
- Never take action when you are angry
- Be willing to lose a battle in order to win a war
- Beware of a person who has nothing to lose
- Don't expect life to be fair
- Do what needs doing when it needs to be done
- Get your priorities straight
- Silence is one of the hardest arguments to refute
- The greatest freedom for ourselves is to free ourselves from fear
- The greatest blessing is good health
- The greatest force is faith in god
- The greatest loss is loss of self-confidence
- The greatest need is common sense
- The real happiness evolves when happiness is shared
- Stay away from bad habits
- Keep yourself happy, healthy, and cheerful

Phone home regularly. Remember, we love you and wait for your call anxiously.

Love,

Maa and Paa

Dear reader, I wish that you seek your calling and fulfill your dreams. I would like to leave you with one of my favorite quotes from a book *Oh! the Places You'll Go* by Dr Seuss.

'You have brains in your head.
You have feet in your shoes.
You can steer yourself any direction you choose.

With your head full of brains and your shoes full of feet,
You're too smart to go down a not-so-good-street.

Out there things can happen, and frequently do,
To people as brainy and footsy as you.
And when things start to happen, don't worry, don't stew.
Just go right along, you'll start happening too!'

# Acknowledgements

I DEDICATE THIS BOOK TO THE almighty and my alma mater IIM Bangalore, where I did the PGSEM programme between 2001 and 2004, and to all students, staff, faculty, alumni and friends of this institute. Each of them had a role to play to help me shape this book. I consider myself a curator and presenter of information created by them and am deeply indebted to all of them for helping me discover myself.

I feel honoured to serve this institute in the capacity of head of alumni and development office, probably the only one of its kind in the country, and as an adjunct faculty of Communication. So I probably am one of those few lucky ones who get to meet a student as soon as they enter the institute and continue engaging with them even after they become alumni of IIMB. On any given day at the institute, I get to meet a number of ex-students. I observe their career graphs, their ways of thinking, and try to learn from them. Most of them are really smart and wonderful people who are capable of becoming world class leaders some day. Every year we do reunions for the batches that complete 10, 15, 20, 25, 30 and 35 years. I enjoy sitting with them, listening to their stories from the day they left campus to where they are now. So as I said earlier, I merely curated the story of a cross section of our alumni who have an ocean of knowledge on how to find one's true calling and managing careers. Special thanks to Arun, Malavika, Ravi, Bhargav, Apurva, Vivek, Haragopal, Rajiv, Deeptha, and Vikash for giving me a chance to document their stories for this book. Each of them spent labourious hours with me for the interviews, and helped me shape the chapters.

While I always wanted to write something about career choices, I must tell the story of how this book happened. It was nothing less than a miracle. It was mid-2012. I had finished teaching my class and was having tea at the corner behind the P cluster of campus. Prabhakar and Rupa, a sweet couple, run this small tuck shop which sustains many of us at the institute through the torturous classes, assignments, and presentations. Some of my students joined in. We were casually discussing the career dilemmas they have and I knew they had a tough terrain in front of them. When you really want to do something, the world conspires to make it happen. I went back to my office and saw an email from Radhika Marwah from Random House asking me if I would like to write a book on how alumni made career choices which could help the students. That did it. I knew that the time had come for me to put all these experiences in a book. Radhika, Milee, thank you for giving me this opportunity to work on this book with you. The team at Random House is lean but can pack a mean wallop. They know what they are doing and I feel comfortable that the book is in good hands. The cover design by Anjora is stunning. I also would like to appreciate the efforts of Caroline and Anindita to make the book known through their marketing and PR efforts.

A big shout out to all my students. They are the real heroes who kept me energized and readily shared their points of view. I wish I could list all their names but that would not be possible given the challenges of real estate in the page. I do want to call out to a few of them who helped me immensely in this journey—Renuka, Sayali, Swapnil, Vaibhav, Milaap, Vijay, Vrinda, Harsan, Vivek, Vallabh, Himen, Monika, Aditi, Siva, Merben, Saurabh, and the entire alumcom and placecom group of IIMB students.

Swaroop and Vivek of Edu-Next, who are also fellow alums from my graduate college NIT Surathkal and IIMB, thank you for the initial research with students from various other colleges of India. This research was immensely useful in the foundation of the book.

A special thank you to Anamika Chakravarty, alumna of PGP '92. Anamika is the founder and partner at Chrysalis which is committed to mindfulness and conscious living. Mindfulness is a non-judgment state of active and open attention to the present, whose benefits include lower stress, better decision making and a sense of greater well-being. She volunteered to spend more than two months of her time to put those career choice boxes in sectors. Her batch and friends also chipped in with inputs of their own experiences based on the sector they were in. I'd also like to thank Arpita Menon, Rajkamal Velampati, Gagan Kumar, Sunil Mehra, Debarjyo Nandi, Kanishka Chowdhary, Stephen Dantas, Karthi Kumar Marshan, Dhiraj Agarwal, Mahendran Balachandran, Anuj Kumar, Gaurav Bakshi, Balasubramanian Sankaramahalingan, Shantanu Ghosh, Sharda Agarwal, Puja Nandi , Sarabjit Sachar, Prakash Bagri, Abhijit Majumdar, and Sandip Roy.

My colleagues at the IIMB Alumni Office – Sushma, Rohini, Aparna, Ranjini, and Gayatri, thank you for taking up all the work on your shoulders and letting me write this book.

Last but not least, I would like to thank my parents, my wife, and my children for being my strength and support.

I pledge my earnings from this book to IIM Bangalore and to The Akshaya Patra Foundation.

# A Note on the Author

Rakesh Godhwani calls himself a nobody. After spending amazing formative years in great organizations in the high-tech space like Wipro, Intel and Qualcomm—doing different roles in sales, product marketing and business development—Rakesh realized that his passion lay in helping others reach their maximum potential and fulfil their dreams.

Rakesh currently heads IIM Bangalore Alumni Association, coaches entrepreneurs and leaders in the hi-tech sector, teaches Managerial Communication and Communication for Leaders at IIM Bangalore, does yoga, cycles his way to work, earns a fraction of what he used to but lives a million times better. Rakesh's first book Plunnge was released in July, 2011. More details can be found on www.plunnge.com or www.facebook.com/plunnge.

Rakesh is an alumnus of KREC (now NITK) Surathkal, class of 1997 and of IIM Bangalore PGSEM, class of 2004.